VGM Professional Careers Series

CAREERS
IN COMPUTERS

LILA B. STAIR

D1416243

VGM Career Horizons
a division of *NTC Publishing Group*
Lincolnwood, Illinois USA

Cover photo courtesy of Hewlett-Packard Company.

Library of Congress Cataloging-in-Publication Data
Stair, Lila B.
    Careers in computers / Lila B. Stair.
        p. cm. — (VGM professional careers series)
    Includes bibliographical references and index.
    ISBN 0-8442-4481-3 (h). — ISBN 0-8442-4482-1 (p)
    1. Computer science—Vocational guidance. 2. Electonic data
processing—Vocational guidance. I. Title.   II. Series.
QA76.25.S67   1996
004'.023—dc20   95-21862
                                                 CIP

Published by VGM Career Horizons, a division of NTC Publishing Group
4255 West Touhy Avenue
Lincolnwood (Chicago), Illinois 60646-1975, U.S.A.

5 6 7 8 9 0 VP 9 8 7 6 5 4 3 2 1

ABOUT THE AUTHOR

Lila Stair is a professional author in the areas of careers and business. She holds an M.A. in counseling from the University of New Orleans and an M.B.A. from Florida State University. As an instructor of business courses at both community college and university levels, she has had an opportunity to both teach business concepts and to assist students in selecting business careers.

Formerly a career counselor, the author has worked with hundreds of students. As well as counseling and providing students with career information, she has worked with employers in job development and placement. In her position as counselor in the Program for the Achievement of Competency Education (PACE), she worked both with employers and community college instructors to write competencies needed for success in various jobs and to develop courses with objectives designed to meet these competencies.

In her capacity as career counselor, the author established career resource centers containing available sources of career information including computerized career information services. Many of these sources are used to research her books. However, her books reflect the most up-to-date trends and career information published in current business journals. To assist individuals in researching and making career choices, the author has developed a model for evaluating careers in terms of aptitudes, interests, and values. This model appears in *Careers in Business* published by the NTC Publishing Group. It has been reprinted in a personnel textbook.

Her continuing dedication to the field of career development began in 1972 in Springfield, Oregon as a counselor in a school district that was a pioneer in career education. This early experience shaped the author's own career emphasis. A recipient of the General Electric Foundation Career Guidance Fellowship, the author spent six weeks at the University of South Carolina exchanging information with counselors from all over the country and gaining ideas in the area of career education. The author feels that the need for accurate up-to-date information exists today as it did then and works to provide this information through her books.

CONTENTS

PREFACE

http://www.occ.com/occ/SearchAllJobs.html will connect job hunters to one of the World Wide Web's most popular spots—the Online Career Center. Internet, the worldwide communications network, has made volumes of valuable, up-to-date information available to both individuals and organizations. Requiring only a personal computer and modem, an individual can for a modest fee access the world. Gophering enables users to seek out information such as tables of statistics and documents from 3,000 to 5,000 gopher sites at universities, government agencies, or large corporations—without first logging in to their computers. Commercial services such as Simon & Schuster's *College Online* offers students tips for writing research papers, *Compton's Encyclopedia, The Library of Congress* for online exhibits around the world, a catalog to locate titles relevant to specific research topics, a variety of current periodicals, information on how to locate information on the Internet, E–mail access to experts in a field of interest, and even career assistance. Information is the key to success in the world today; computers and communications networks are the vehicles offering access.

Computer careers offer variety, money, challenge, and numerous job opportunities. Rapidly changing technology and major innovations in computer programming cause jobs in computer related fields to change as well. Some knowledge and training becomes quickly obsolete as demand surges for individuals with specific skills in new techniques and technologies. By acquiring the kind of information available in this book, careful career planning, and keeping aware of new developments in computer fields, one can be in a position to take advantage of the many opportunities available in computer careers.

Computers are visible in almost every aspect of our daily lives. The computer revolution is not about machines but rather the movement and management of massive amounts of information. Many of today's offices have more personal computers than people. Some level of computer training is required for most jobs today. Computer technology has made possible advances in equipment, techniques, and research in every area of our personal and organizational lives. Computer professionals have a broad range of interests and experience, and there are endless possibilities for developing those interests within the job market today.

WHO SHOULD READ THIS BOOK?

This book is written for anyone interested in working with computers. The range of jobs described in the book is very broad and includes jobs in information departments in organizations, with computer manufacturers, and as entrepreneurs or freelance consultants and program contractors. The Job Index lists job titles for the positions discussed in this book. A special chapter on opportunities for women, teens, elderly, minorities, and the physically challenged provides additional information for these groups.

PRACTICAL INFORMATION

As well as job descriptions, this book will include salary data, present and future job market information, personal and educational requirements for those entering computer careers, essential job-seeking skills, tips on planning a career, and many sources of additional information for both job seekers and professionals. Computer trends and their effect on careers will also be discussed. In short, all types of information to help plan for and succeed in a computer career will be included.

ACKNOWLEDGMENTS

Much of the information for this book was provided by my strongest advocate, Ralph Stair, author of *Principles of Information Systems*, published by Boyd & Fraser, and numerous other books in the computer field. His enthusiasm for computers is highly contagious, was passed on to me, and will hopefully be spread to you who read this book.

Lila B. Stair

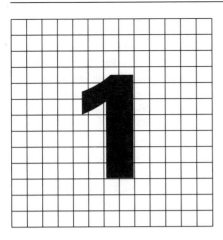

WORKING WITH COMPUTERS TODAY AND IN THE FUTURE

Futurists look to the workplace of year 2000 and see a computational infrastructure with computers at its heart. Technology has redefined the structure of organizations, the way we do business, the types of jobs we hold, and the nature of work itself. The average company will be smaller and employ fewer people. Such companies as IBM, Digital Equipment, AT&T, companies central to the new infrastructure, have been getting smaller. A study by Professors Erik Brynjolfsson and Thomas W. Malone of MIT found that the typical company has eliminated 20 percent of its employees and has tripled its investment in information technology over the past ten years. Networks and newly skilled users will lessen the need for centralized technology functions. Information professionals will be assigned to business units in increasing numbers where they will need greater knowledge of the business. Those left in the information center will assume roles of consultant, systems integrator, and network manager. Fewer management levels and more teams are characteristic of both today's and tomorrow's corporations. Technicians and specialists will be the most common job titles.

The revolution in the workplace was started by the development of the microprocessor—a chip no bigger than a fingernail—which enabled the computerization of so many activities in our world. The early computer was composed of a room filled with bulky equipment. Its speed was slow, its use was limited, and, for most purposes, it's cost was prohibitive. Then came the technology of microelectronics. Today that roomful of equipment can fit into the palm of your hand. The computer is faster, cheaper, more sophisticated, and infinitely more versatile than its predecessor. The computer has become a household word, if not an addition. In 1994, Americans spent roughly $9 billion on nearly 7 million home computers, 40 percent of all personal computers sold in the United States. Projections are that the home will become

1

the biggest market for personal computers by the year 2000, outpacing sales to businesses. Scenarios vary regarding how the computer will impact our lives in the future just as individual lifestyles vary, but one fact is certain: computers will perform the more mundane operations in our lives, saving us time and energy and increasing our possibilities for work and leisure.

To some extent people today must be computer literate, that is, they must have the ability to communicate through computers in order to function both in their jobs, whatever the field, and in society. Computer literacy is taught in schools beginning in primary grades and continuing through high school where computer labs have become common. Even three-year-old preschoolers are enjoying such delightful programs as "Ugly Bug," and they are using the computer handily when they reach kindergarten. Today more and more schools use high speed computers linked to on-line services in the classroom and stress the acquisition of information. Electronic games like Nintendo and Sega Genesis are on innumerable Christmas lists. Students today are as much at ease with computer keyboards and screens as students of the 1950s were with typewriters.

The computer is permeating almost every workplace. Many jobs have been eliminated, others changed, and new ones created. Many routine clerical jobs have been eliminated, and created in their place new, better paid positions in the growing information-systems field. The increased use of robots in industry has displaced many manufacturing workers. Jobs created through the expanded use of robots require technical skills not always easy for the unskilled or semiskilled worker to obtain.

Computerization has required retraining many people, adjusting to change which is not easy, and filling new positions for which there are shortages of qualified individuals. Thus there are both positive and negative aspects of the computer revolution. But to those entering the newer, better paid positions born from computerization, it is easy to focus on the positive.

COMPUTER USE: HISTORY AND HIGHLIGHTS

The computer got its start in government work in the compilation of the 1890 census and continues to be used for that purpose. Today massive databases characterize many of the government's operations: for example, the Internal Revenue Service. Computers dominate Pentagon activities, and the computer is at the heart of nuclear defense. The space program would still be in the realm of science fiction without the help of the computer.

Computers have been on the cutting edge of science and technology over the past few decades. In medicine the computer made news when Nan Davis, a 22-year-old paraplegic, walked for the first time in over four years with the help of computer-generated electrical impulses. Essentially the computer simulated her brain's activity by giving commands to the leg muscles through electrodes wired to her legs. The results of the pioneering work of Jerrold Petrofsky, a biomedical engineer, and his Wright State University team are history. A new field called computer-stimulated rehabilitation points out once again the host of possibilities available to those who work with computers. Today scientists are using advanced computer graphics and virtual reality to develop three-dimensional images to help surgeons operate. Software has been developed to help surgeons locate and remove the epileptic focus which causes seizures. Intraoral video cameras are being used by dentists to record and project images which are then logged as digital files into a database. Pharmacists are using computers to design drugs. The list goes on and on.

The computer has been widely used for producing art, music, special effects in films, and the ever-popular video games. The potential of the computer for artistic purposes is being realized by moviemakers. In the early 1980s, the film *Tron* caused a stir when approximately sixteen minutes of the one-hundred-minute movie used computer-generated animation and another forty-five minutes used 150 computer-drawn backgrounds and sets. In total, over one-third of *Tron* was generated by computer. In 1989, an Academy Award was given to a totally computer-generated animated film of a baby playing with his toys. Today it is possible to film a scene, change it within the computer, and scan the altered images back onto file—with the changes undetectable. Warner has already produced a series of CDs that store audio and data. The first, Mozart's opera *The Magic Flute*, can be played like a regular music CD or hooked up to an Apple MacIntosh for written commentary timed to the singing. Today, CD–ROM drives are built into many computers. Multimedia encyclopedias, live-action games, and scads of educational material are available. That's *infotainment*!

The computer has made an impact in the sports arena. The National Football League teams use computers to provide instant data. Computers are programmed to diagram and analyze offensive and defensive plays of both teams and their opponents. For a pre-game analysis, the computer analyzes an opposing team's offensive and defensive plays from the last few games and predicts what the opponent will do in specific situations. The computer also is used in the design of football equipment to reduce the chance of permanent paralysis or brain damage to players. To do this it is programmed to analyze films during which an injury takes place and to produce graphs showing the force in pounds absorbed at points of the player's body at certain points in time. Yet another use of the computer in sports is biomechanics. A familiar concept in Russian and East German athletics since the early 1960s, the computer is used in the United States as well to coach its Olympic athletes. A microcomputer is programmed to watch athletes and tell them how to improve their techniques. The computer draws attention to factors too subtle to be detected by the human coach.

Database systems are invaluable in crime fighting. Information on criminals, stolen vehicles, and missing persons is readily available. The Missing Children Act created a centralized child database to help local and state law enforcement authorities locate and identify the nearly two million children reported missing each year. The act also provided for the creation of a database of unidentified dead bodies to help eliminate the uselessness of a family spending its life savings to search for a missing child whose body has already turned up in another state. Leonard Rubin, Management Information Systems Director for the New York County district attorney's office, has computerized a portion of the work of the prosecutor. Software has been developed that automatically fills in the proper legal language when an entry clerk types a certain code. Substituting for the polygraph, Verimetrics Systems, Inc., sells a computer that "reads" a voice to detect the stress produced by lying and to produce a voice print, which is as unique in individuals as are fingerprints. The latest in ID technology is software that captures facial thermograms (systems of blood vessels), which like fingerprints are distinct in each individual, that can be read using an infrared camera, a computer, and a database.

These computer applications are but a few highlights to demonstrate how the computer has advanced from its early clerical uses to extend across many fields. Computer professionals are directly responsible for some of the exciting outcomes described above. With the coming of the second computer age, there are now computers that reason, make judgments, and learn. Such artificial intelligence enables computers to diagnose diseases, locate mineral deposits, determine where to drill oil wells, prepare income tax returns, give investment advice, and perform a variety of other "thinking" activities. Tomorrow's developments promise to be even more interesting than today's as advancing technology continues to exceed everyone's expectations.

COMPUTERS IN THE 1990s

While technological innovations have continued beyond most futurists' wildest dreams over the past decade, state-of-the-art computer technology has realized only a fraction of its potential. The dilemma is how to transfer technology from the research and development lab to a development team and finally into the hands of users. Incorporating the new technology into a company's manufacturing process and marketing program requires resources (such as funds) to devote to the project and personnel with the appropriate skills and experience to pull it off. The wheels of large corporations grind very slowly when it comes to committing such resources to new products. For this reason, new companies bankrolled by venture capitalists have introduced much of the existing technology to the marketplace, and many of the ideas generated in the research and development labs of large companies remain on the drawing board.

Many experts believe that the next ten years will be characterized by better use of existing technologies rather than technological breakthroughs. The new technologies introduced in the 1980s have shaped computing and impacted computer careers in the 1990s, including improved personal computer and workstation technologies, expert systems in the area of artificial intelligence, local-area networks (LAN) and wide-area networks (WAN) in the field of communications, computer-aided software engineering (CASE), and imaging systems in the field of optical technology.

Personal Computers

Over the 1980s, improvements in personal computer technology caused an explosion in their numbers and uses. Personal computers became smaller, with laptop sales growing at twice the rate of desktop personal computers. Today notebooks and subnotebooks weighing between three and four pounds are claiming their share of the market. The power of the personal computer has grown and rivals that of the more powerful workstations, which are enhanced microcomputers that have stand-alone capabilities, electronic mail capabilities, and communications access with the main computer. The trend is toward smaller yet more powerful personal computers, and the technology is in place. Software development has begun to catch up with the hardware, offering an ever-wider variety of applications and competing products. Software development in the future will focus on facilitating collaboration among colleagues. A whole new generation of network software will link people in remote locations. It will become easier to use and obtain customer support. PCs of the future will feature larger screens to take advantage of better graphics and will use windows capable of running many programs at a time. New peripherals will become available, such as small cameras for teleconferencing and optical scanners for digitizing images. The PC will become a message center for voice mail, faxes, and E–mail complete with video clips.

The increase in personal-computer use in organizations has given birth to a new job, the personal computer manager. In addition, the increased number of computer users has resulted in active user groups who demand to be involved in the development of the tools they need and will ultimately use. Such groups as the Chicago Association for Microcomputer Professionals (CAMP) and the Microcomputer Managers Association (MMA) in New York are providing computer vendors with feedback on existing products and the requirements that meet the needs of personal computer professionals. This involvement has changed the nature of systems development and the jobs of the computer professionals employed both within the computer industry and in companies with information systems departments.

Supercomputers

Large computer systems costing from five- to twenty-million dollars enable the military and research and development teams to tackle complex problems and to extend knowledge. These computers offer faster processing speeds than any other computer system. Used by large companies and universities for research purposes, these computers are the exception to the rule that everything is getting smaller.

Expert Systems

Despite the skeptical reception of artificial intelligence a few years ago, such diverse industries as utilities, chemicals, transportation, electronics, health care, and process manufacturing are developing and using expert systems. The systems are designed to simulate thinking of experts in the field to provide "intelligent" information to be used in decision making. As always, the limits of the new technology initially were misunderstood. The expert system is designed not to replace but rather to assist the expert. For example, SUMEX, an early artificial intelligence system developed years ago, imitates the thought processes of the physician. It is programmed to match signs and symptoms, suggest diagnoses, and provide information on drugs. Today railroads are developing expert systems to perform better derailment and accident analysis modeling. Utility companies are using expert systems to determine when to purchase the oil, gas, and uranium for electricity production. Almost every industry can offer examples of expert systems development or use. The delay in the introduction of expert systems is due in part to the lack of individuals in systems analysis and programming who possess the skills to produce such systems. These computer professionals, called knowledge engineers, are among the most wanted by corporations today.

Networks

The field of communications has had a dramatic effect on computer technology. Banks, airlines, retail stores, and numerous other consumer industries use computer terminals for on-line transaction processing (OLTP). The system of electronic pathways that connects these terminals with a central or main computer is called a *network*. A network covering a broad geographical area is called a *wide area network* (WAN). A network confined to one building or office complex is called a *local area network* (LAN). More widespread use of personal computers has greatly contributed to the establishment of LANs. Networks now link together PCs, minicomputers, and mainframes giving users access to vast information sources. Initially, personal computers were used by individuals only to increase their personal productivity. As more people within a company got personal computers, the desire to use them to communicate with each other electronically arose. Thus the concept of electronic mail (E–mail) began to be used internally. It was far easier and quicker to send a memo electronically than through the office mail. The Electronic Messaging Service reported that about fifteen million workers in *Fortune* 2,000 companies were using E–mail in 1994.

Personal computers can be connected to the main computer, printers, and copy machines for direct access to data files and equipment housed in a central place in the building. Thus LANs provide a more efficient and productive way for company employees to perform their jobs, share information, and communicate throughout the organization without ever leaving their offices. Such office computer networks have created a demand for a new type of software called *groupware* to improve communications and coordinate work activities. Advances in communications technology will provide LANs for multimedia workstations that allow not only transmission of print and graphics but voice, video, and even three-dimensional animated digital graphics as well.

Internet, the international network that allows communications via computer, is currently used by 20- to 30-million people. If Internet continues its current growth rate, it is estimated that 40 million people will have access to it by 1996. Internet offerings continue to expand, including tax tips, scientific facts, political current affairs, sports news, even live broadcasts such as twenty minutes of the Rolling Stones Dallas concert. New state-of-the-art software is available that allows users to bypass traditional telephones in making long-distance calls around the world.

Computer-Aided Software Engineering (CASE)

Computer-aided software engineering (CASE) tools are software packages used to generate code according to parameters specified by programmers. CASE tools can greatly reduce the time required by programmers to generate new programs and to revise old ones. The greatest cost in information systems is in programming because of the time required to write and debug programs. For this reason, many companies began to use independent contractors to develop programs or packaged software. Off-the-shelf software does not always work well for highly specific applications and still must be modified to serve the company's purposes. The new CASE tools enable organizations to once again develop their own software without the tremendous cost and time commitments of the past.

While CASE tools rarely eliminate the job of the programmer, they do modify it and reduce programmer time. In large operations, this often eliminates programmer jobs. In time, as the tools are improved and become more user friendly, individuals other than programmers may be able to generate programs without formal training in programming. The demand for application programmers has already declined as the software industry continues to produce more and better software packages. If the potential of CASE tools is realized, this decline will be even greater. On the other hand, there will be many opportunities within the software industry itself for programmers with the skills to produce state-of-the-art programs.

Imaging Systems

Banking, insurance, transportation, health care, and petroleum industries are enthusiastic about the advances in imaging systems. These systems enable documents to be digitized and shared across large networks. Faster and easier retrieval of documents in paper-intensive industries provides the key to efficiency. The associated area of optical storage reduces the space required to house company records. Optical disks and other high density storage devices are also more convenient to access than microfilm and microfiche. Like the other new technologies, imaging systems and optical storage have great potential. A *gigabyte* is roughly equivalent to seven hundred books with an average of four hundred pages each, not counting pictures. It is estimated that within five years a storage device containing a gigabyte of data will fit in a shirt pocket.

The Impact of Changing Technology on Companies

Information systems directors are overwhelmed by the variety of new products on the market. To be competitive, a company must be as productive as the competition. Information systems can provide the means for improved productivity. To lag behind technologically is to lose one's competitive edge. The problem is to select the best tools to make use of the new technologies. For this reason many companies form advanced technology groups (ATGs) or teams of people assigned the task of studying the new technologies and recommending the best ways to implement them in the organization. The decisions made by information managers affect the roles of computer professionals within their organizations.

Computers are the tools that generate information, but information is the resource that is shaping the future. In corporations today the emphasis is on information services rather than on computer systems. This move from the technical to the applied has changed the nature and title of many jobs, the demand for certain skills, and the very terminology of the field. *Information systems* (IS) has replaced *data processing* (DP) to show the broader scope of both computer technology and applications. As CASE technologies gain in popularity, programmers will do less coding and will be referred to as software engineers, already the preferred job title within the computer industry. As you will see in Figure 1.1, the extended size and scope of the information function in today's organizations has resulted in more departments than ever before.

The Issue of Privacy

A major concern today is how the growth of computer and data communications affects our privacy. Protecting an individual's privacy in the Information Age while not impinging upon the freedoms of others in the quest for information is a tricky issue. Data on individuals exists in various databases without their knowledge or consent. Unwanted junk mail and phone calls, even electronic junk mail, are a nuisance. Numerous bills have been proposed, among them a bill creating a national privacy commission to oversee enforcement of the Privacy Act of 1974 that requires federal agencies to adhere to a set of rules governing the collection, maintenance, use, and dissemination of information on an individual. Another bill orders the FCC to conduct a privacy survey of the new technologies and limits the use of Customer Propriety Number Information. According to the President's Domestic Council Committee on the Right of Privacy, one-third to one-half of the gross national product of the United States can be attributed to the production of information and knowledge. The issue of who owns this information and who is entitled to access to it is an extremely complex one. Knowledge workers and users can expect to deal with invasion of privacy problems along with computer waste, crime, and various other security issues in the future.

THE WORK OF INFORMATION PROFESSIONALS

Computers are used at every level of most organizations. From management decision making to simple record keeping, billing, payroll, and inventory control applications, computers play a valuable role in businesses. Science labs use computers in research. Automated equipment is common in manufacturing plants. Executives are rarely without their desktop computers as they call up the information required to make complicated and crucial decisions. In grocery stores and other retail outlets, computerized scanners enable quicker service and better inventory control. The banking and airline industries have been computer dependent in almost every aspect of their operations for years.

Computer professionals may be employed in a variety of jobs by almost any type of organization or within the computer industry and data services industries. The types of jobs held by computer professionals fall into several general categories: computer design and manufacture, computer sales and service, systems development and software engineering, and computer operations.

Computer Design and Manufacture

Employed by computer manufacturers are the scientists, mathematicians, engineers, and technicians who research, design, and produce the equipment (hardware) and the programs (software) to make it work. It all begins with these professionals.

Computer Sales and Service

Once the hardware and software are developed, they must be marketed, sold, and serviced by a vendor representative, an individual specializing in business systems or scientific applications. A vendor representative serves as a liaison between the computer vendor and the purchasing organization. Once the system is sold, the field engineer installs the hardware and software and then services it periodically to keep it running smoothly.

Systems Development and Software Engineering

This category includes such jobs as systems analyst and programmer. These jobs involve the development of systems along with sets of instructions (software) to serve a variety of purposes in business, science, entertainment, and other fields. Software may be produced by computer vendors and sold along with the hardware or it may be produced in-house, in both cases by computer professionals in systems development and software engineering.

Computer Operations

The computer professionals in operations work closely with the systems development and programming personnel. They enter data into the computer and operate the equipment. The work of word processing personnel is an important part of operations.

Figure 1.1   Information Systems Organization Chart

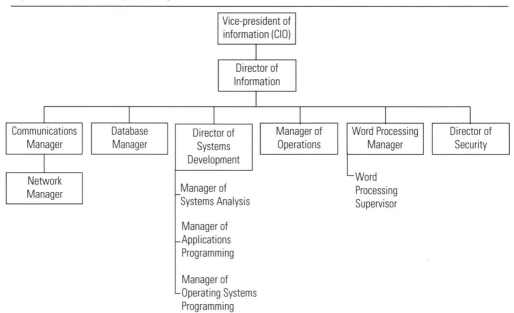

CAREERS IN AN INFORMATION SYSTEMS DEPARTMENT

Computer-based information systems are a combination of hardware, software, databases, telecommunications, procedures, and the people who use the technology to input, process, and output the information needed to run an organization. Computer professionals are employed in a variety of jobs within the information systems department of an organization. How these positions are organized or how many specialized positions exist depends on the philosophy and size of the organization. Figure 1.1 is a sample chart of the information systems function of an organization.

Chapter 2 describes the work of computer professionals involved in the areas of systems development. It includes descriptions of numerous specialists. The levels at which individuals work at different stages of their career development and how individuals with different functions work together will be described. As you can see from the chart, these systems development professionals are part of the information systems department of an organization. Also playing vital roles in systems development are the applications and operating systems programmers whose jobs are discussed in Chapter 3. Included in the information systems department are the operations and word processing center personnel who are described in Chapter 4. Specialists in telecommunications, networks, and data security are discussed in Chapter 5. The complex jobs of information executives are explained in Chapter 7.

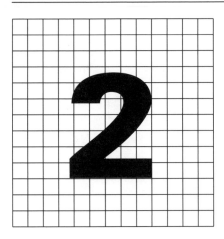

CAREERS IN SYSTEMS DEVELOPMENT

Systems development has as a field undergone radical change in recent years. Large flexible systems include not only the traditional mainframes but up to hundreds of small computers or workstations connected by networks to one another and to specialized "server" computers that manage databases, print jobs, house electronic mail, and so on. Systems and software development have been assisted by computer-aided software engineering (CASE) tools. The new systems and components facilitate the location and generation of information crucial to the advancement of science, to the growth of industry, to the management of business, to the operation of the government—in fact, to the improvement of every aspect of our daily lives.

The development of systems containing sets of instructions (*software*) by which the computer machinery and equipment (*hardware*) is used for problem solving requires people who understand both the problem and the computer's capabilities. These people are employed in the areas of systems development and programming. Chapter 2 will discuss jobs in systems development, stressing, in particular, systems analysis, the best known of these jobs. Chapter 3 will describe jobs in programming and related areas. Although programming is a vital part of systems development in the broader sense, it is an area with a separate manager and enough job opportunities and position descriptions to justify a chapter of its own.

Systems development is governed by demands from end users who must get results in a rapidly changing, highly competitive business environment. In the past, systems development was similar to building a house. A systems analyst assumed the role of architect conferring with end users (homeowners) about their wants and needs. The systems designer was the contractor and the coders or programmers were the tradespeople who built the system according to specification. Users were involved only in the analysis stage and as the final recipients of

Figure 2.1   Systems Development Life Cycle

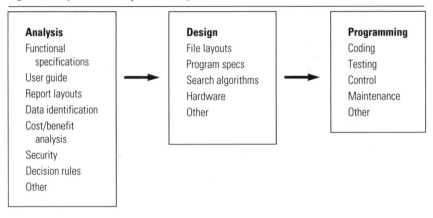

the product. However, in systems development a substantial time period can elapse between analysis and end use, resulting in an out-of-date system when it is finally available. For this reason systems development today involves end users in every stage of the systems development life cycle, which is shown in Figure 2.1. A phenomenon exists in systems analysis that contributes to turnover regardless of the job market situation. The services of the systems analyst are in heavy demand during the development stage of a systems project. After systems are implemented, the modification and maintenance period begins. The services of the systems analyst are required less and less, thus the popular expression: "Competent systems analysts are always building themselves out of jobs." The systems analyst then tends to move to a new project or, in some cases, to a new firm. Today, unlike the beginning of the computer revolution when computers were scarce, computers are readily available both to those in systems development and to end users. Therefore, both groups can work closely together throughout the development life cycle. Using some of the new LAN and CASE technologies described in Chapter 1, electronic commands can be reviewed and altered at each step in systems development to conform to changing conditions in the user environment. Systems development is a team effort involving analysts, technicians, and subject matter experts.

This chapter will include the basic roles of systems development personnel as well as more specific functions and job titles at various stages in an individual's career. Systems development includes a wide range of activities such as investigation, analysis, design, programming, implementation, and maintenance of information systems within an organization.

THE ROLE OF SYSTEMS ANALYSTS

The systems analyst is a professional problem solver. The job involves first analyzing problems or informational needs within an organization, and then

Figure 2.2   What Makes a System

- System name and short description
- Physical considerations: geography and equipment
- Functions: tasks, timing, and algorithms
- Data: flows and characteristics
- Organization: management and support
- Costs
- Problems and opportunities
- Interfaces to other systems and organizations
- Critical success factors for the business and the system
- Documentation: technical and user
- Staff: technical and user
- Training: materials and personnel
- Restrictions

designing efficient patterns of information flow from data sources to the computer to solve them. The systems analyst also plans the distribution of information based on how it is to be used within the organization. In order to design and maintain a reliable and efficient system of information flow, the systems analyst works closely with managers, accountants, and other user groups within the organization to determine their informational needs or their problems. An understanding of how various areas in the organization operate, such as accounting and marketing, and the ability to communicate effectively with coworkers in these areas are crucial to the effectiveness of the systems analyst. Whether the problem is monitoring the environment inside a space shuttle or designing an inventory control system for a business, the ability to communicate with those who use the information generated by the system is essential.

The work of the systems analyst may be to design a new system or to improve an existing one. A system is a collection of people, machines, programs, and procedures organized to perform a certain task. Figure 2.2 is a checklist of the components of a system. Analysts use such techniques as cost accounting, sampling, and mathematical model building to design a system. This is followed by the development of flowcharts, graphs, and diagrams that describe how the system will work.

The systems analyst then relates the requirements of the system to the capabilities of the computer hardware and prepares specifications for programmers to follow in developing the software to make the system work. In small organizations the systems analysts may do the programming themselves. Systems analysts usually spend a couple of years as programmers before being promoted to this position.

There are a number of basic skills needed by systems analysts, as well as the specific technical knowledge of their field and an understanding of the functions of their organization. It is extremely important that systems analysts

Figure 2.3 System Analysis Career Path

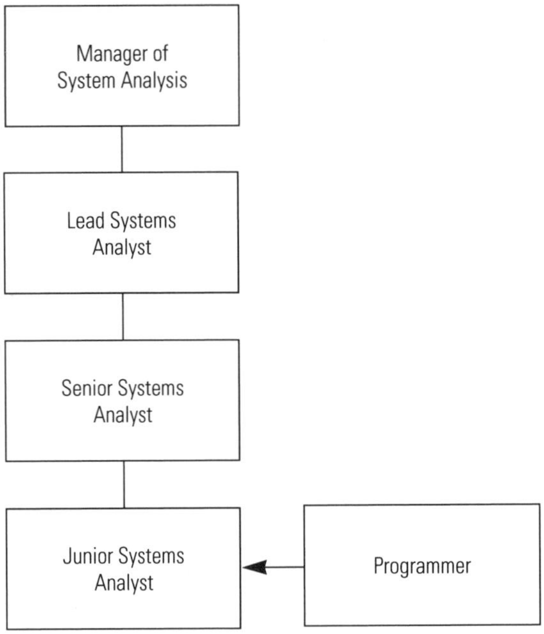

```
                    ┌─────────────────────┐
                    │     Manager of      │
                    │   System Analysis   │
                    └─────────────────────┘
                              │
                    ┌─────────────────────┐
                    │    Lead Systems     │
                    │      Analyst        │
                    └─────────────────────┘
                              │
                    ┌─────────────────────┐
                    │   Senior Systems    │
                    │      Analyst        │
                    └─────────────────────┘
                              │
         ┌─────────────────────┐      ┌─────────────────────┐
         │   Junior Systems    │◄─────│     Programmer      │
         │      Analyst        │      │                     │
         └─────────────────────┘      └─────────────────────┘
```

be willing and able to communicate effectively with others. Also, an ability for problem solving is necessary to reduce problems to an elementary level, define component parts, develop alternative and innovative solutions, analyze advantages and disadvantages of these solutions, and select the best alternative. Since most systems analysts have some supervisory or management duties, management skills such as estimating, scheduling, controlling time, maintaining efficient work habits, and accepting responsibility are important.

Computer-aided software engineering (CASE) is a collection of computer-based systems development tools designed to assist in all aspects of systems development. Upper–CASE tools assist with early stages in systems development such as data-flow diagrams, layout designs, and data dictionaries. Lower–CASE tools focus on the implementation stage and can automatically generate structured code. CASE products are available for personal computers, networks, and mainframe computer systems. These systems development tools are expensive, but experts feel that they can substantially reduce costs and save time compared to nonautomated systems development.

CAREER LEVELS IN SYSTEMS ANALYSIS

To clarify the need for management skills, note the various career levels in Figure 2.3. Although systems analysis career paths can vary depending on the size of the organization and the way the information systems department is organized, the figure gives an idea of the various levels at which an individual might work in a medium-sized organization. In a larger organization there would be more levels between trainee and senior analyst. The manager of systems analysis is in full charge. This individual may personally supervise the operations of the systems analysis area or may delegate this to a subordinate. Responsibilities include the overall analysis of how information systems technologies can be applied to user problems through the design of efficient and effective systems. This requires the integration of systems analysis activities and the various functional areas of the organization. Usually a minimum of five years of systems development experience and some management duties are required for this position. It can lead to information systems management. The lead analyst is essentially the assistant manager, functioning in place of the manager in case of his or her absence. In addition to performing supervisory duties and assisting in planning, organizing, and controlling the activities of the systems analysis section, the lead analyst also may perform technical tasks.

The senior analyst works at the highest technical level of an activity. Typical responsibilities include liaison with users, systems specification and design, and project control. The senior analyst may supervise analysts and programmers until a system is implemented and may occasionally assist in programming. The minimum requirements for this position usually include two years of systems design experience, some programming experience, and specialized industry or organizational experience.

Systems analysts work with users to define the project or some aspect of it and to work out details in specification. The amount of supervision given any analyst depends on the amount of experience. It varies from direct to general supervision. The junior systems analyst usually has a couple of years of programming experience, but he or she may be hired right out of college. At first, the junior systems analyst will spend a good deal of time learning rather than producing. Often this is a probationary position.

Although these descriptions are simplified to some extent, they do reflect the varying degrees of supervision and responsibility experienced by the systems analyst along the well-traveled career path. As systems analysts gain experience, they tend to move into management. It is clear that as systems analysts move from one career level to the next, more time is devoted to supervisory and management duties. Thus the move into management is a transition rather than an abrupt move. Those analysts beyond age fifty who choose to stay in systems analysis or are not promotable to top management hit a salary plateau. Turnover is frequent in this area. Many systems analysts advance by changing companies, gaining a hefty pay hike in the process.

Each organization defines its specific needs. The information systems department and systems development area are organized according to these needs. Consequently, the design of information systems departments will vary substantially even in organizations of comparable size. Chapter 7, devoted entirely to management, will give an indication of paths into top management.

SPECIALIZED AREAS OF SYSTEMS DEVELOPMENT

There are a number of specialized functions performed by those in the broader area of systems development. For example, a systems design analyst may design a number of alternative systems according to the system requirements drawn up by the analyst. From these the best is then chosen. A management information systems analyst works specifically to provide decision-making information to management through the development and implementation of information systems. The operations research analyst solves difficult problems in systems analysis through the use of mathematical techniques. A methods and procedures analyst develops and implements improved clerical methods as part of the development of new or improved systems. A network analyst designs the integration of system communications components.

In general, the larger the information systems department of the organization, the more specialized the positions. More examples of this specialization include systems maintenance and systems support activities. Systems maintenance analysts are responsible for monitoring the information systems once they are implemented. They determine when changes are needed in the system and refer the matter to analysis and design personnel. Systems support analysts perform a variety of activities that support systems development; for example, preparing and updating organization charts, designing forms, managing records, and preparing and distributing corporate policies and procedures. The areas of systems maintenance and systems support may have their own managers, depending on the size of the organization.

Because of the costs associated with new systems development, many companies choose to convert their existing systems to accommodate the new technology. This sometimes requires systems professionals with mastery of more than one *hardware platform* (type of computer equipment), *operating system* (software that runs the basic operations of the computer), or programming language. Rarely do in-house people have such knowledge or ability. Companies turn then to consulting firms that employ conversion specialists. Such individuals with three years of experience can earn $33,000 a year. Systems analysts with five or more years of conversion experience sometimes earn more than $50,000 a year.

Today many companies are undertaking massive systems overhauls to decentralize their applications and take advantage of network technologies. This decentralization results in easier access to information, more efficient service, and quicker response to the market. New networks and databases at the user level might be involved.

What kind of systems professionals are required to pull this off? Wizards, witch doctors, and magicians, new job titles for the star performers in what the Index Group, a Boston consulting organization, calls a "starship environment." The witch doctor is an analyst who has a thorough understanding of the company's business and whose mission is to redesign and revitalize the organization. Magicians, experienced in large-scale systems development, are charged with building cross-functional corporate systems. Wizards, then, are experts on the leading edge of technology who carry out the applied research necessary to bring life to the system.

Some systems analysts specialize in certain types of systems. Database systems, client–server systems, and expert systems are described below.

Database Systems

The database concept was developed as information technology became widely accepted and the need for information increased. A database is a set of related data used by systems analysts and programmers to produce the information needed for the organization to operate. Rather than having numerous data files, each used by only a few people, relevant data are collected in a database to avoid a duplication of efforts in collection, organization, and storage. An organization may maintain more than one database. Databases are housed in the information center.

Whenever a substantial quantity of data must be stored, processed, or retrieved, database analysts and programmers are needed. They are employed in such areas as business, banking, science, or government; any area in which computers are used. Database analysts are also hired by software consulting firms who assist clients in the support of major, sophisticated database systems development. Those specialists in greatest demand are those with exposure to a major CODASYL, or hierarchical database package, and a knowledge of networks. Experience is at a premium and employers will pay dearly for it. A database analyst may move into the position of database administrator in an organization.

It is the job of the database administrator to analyze the company's information requirements, coordinate data collection, organize data into usable databases, store data for efficient access by analysts and programmers, keep databases up-to-date, and establish rules pertaining to the databases and their security. There are languages associated with databases so that data may be accessed more easily and may be added, deleted, or modified. The database administrator trains and assists programmers and nonprogramming users in the use of these languages.

Since the accuracy of the database is crucial to the value of the information derived from its programs, only highly qualified individuals are given the position of database administrator. Usually three to seven years of experience in systems programming and data communications, and a B.S. or B.A. degree in business, mathematics, or computer science are required. A database administrator may supervise a number of database analysts and ultimately advance to the position of database manager.

The size of the database determines the number of database professionals who work under the administrator to perform the duties described above. They are programmers and analysts, with backgrounds in programming and systems methodologies, whose duties are to design database-oriented application systems.

In addition, knowledge of systems software is valuable for persons involved in planning physical database structures and maintaining the security of these structures.

Also working under the database administrator are librarians. The database librarian maintains a library of magnetic tapes, disks, and cartridges. The librarian inspects tapes for wear, replaces those that are worn-out, erases tapes with data that are no longer needed and creates new tapes, disks, or cartridges. The ability to store hundreds, even thousands, of tapes and to locate them quickly when needed is essential to the job.

Today many organizations operate formal information centers to help coordinate end-user computing. A number of organizations also have executive support centers to assist executives in obtaining the information needed to make decisions vital to the organization. These information and executive support centers require personnel with a high level of personal communications skills. They work with employees at all levels of the organization including top management. Specific duties in addition to information system support might include researching competitors, the market, or governmental regulations.

Client–Server Systems

Client–server systems (CCSs) connect the computers of users (clients) to one or more host computers (servers); CCSs can tie personal computers, mainframe systems, databases, and various networks into one integrated and powerful network. A 1994 estimate was that 65 percent of large corporations were already using client–server systems. The use of workstation and personal computer networks by millions of workers created the need for specialists who provide support for these workers. A manager is responsible for implementing client–server systems within the organization. The use of these systems has improved the productivity of many workers, made PC users an integral part of the information function, and created jobs in user support.

Expert Systems

Artificial intelligence, once the subject of science fiction, is now an established field within computer careers. Can computers think? No, but they can simulate thinking through the use of *expert systems*. Expert systems are designed to help (not to replace) decision makers in a wide range of industries. Basically they enable the computer to approximate human judgment through a knowledge base or system of related concepts just as a database generates information based on sets of related facts. The technology works; expert systems would be available for a wider variety of uses if only there were more people with the ability to design them and program the software according to the complicated specifications.

Expert systems design and development, called *knowledge engineering,* is a relatively new field with numerous opportunities. Qualified knowledge engineers are rare for a couple of reasons. First, this highly specialized work requires individuals who understand the infrastructure of the business, possess strong skills in structured interview techniques, and are talented programmers as well. Second, the non-procedural, intuitive nature of knowledge acquisition is contrary to the precise-thinking skills of most competent analysts and programmers. Therefore, job candidates in the field of knowledge engineering are more likely to come from liberal arts rather than computer science backgrounds.

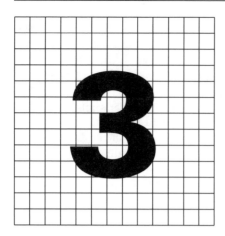

CAREERS IN PROGRAMMING

OOP—object-oriented programming—is becoming a widely used programming tool. Compared to a Tinkertoy, OOP is a set of self-contained modules of standardized pre-written code that allows programmers to plug them into large programs as needed. This greatly simplifies writing hundreds of thousands of lines of interconnected commands. Today's PCs are becoming so powerful that realizing their capacity requires lengthy complex programs. For many applications, OOP is the answer.

Software development is the key to unlocking the potential of computer hardware, which has become less expensive and more powerful over the years. Software can be as much as 75 percent of the total cost of an information system partly because of the time it takes to develop the complex software demanded today. For this reason highly qualified programmers are much in demand and their salaries have increased because of the vital role they play. Operating systems software such as "Windows" by Microsoft is continually revised to compete with new products on the market such as IBM's "Warp."

Professionals in programming positions tell the computer what to do through the programs or sets of instructions that they write. A computer can only do what it has been programmed to do, so without these individuals the machine is nothing but a mass of metal and electronic circuitry. Careers in programming allow for variety and creativity but require very logical people who are attentive to detail and oriented toward perfection.

The application development area includes systems analysts and application programmers and has its own manager. There is not always a clear line between programming and systems analysis, since many individuals perform the functions of both. This is particularly true in small firms. The responsibilities of a programmer/analyst in a small firm are a combination of those of the systems analyst described in Chapter 2 and the duties described below.

THE ROLE OF COMPUTER PROGRAMMERS

The work of computer programmers or software engineers, as they are called in the computer industry, involves writing detailed sets of instructions according to the problem descriptions and specifications of the systems analysts. These programs are made up of a series of logical steps that the machine must follow in order for the data to be processed and transformed into usable information. The programmer may use any one of a number of programming languages: COBOL, FORTRAN, and BASIC are among the older, more common languages. Today, 65 percent of corporate systems still run on COBOL. Programmers should gain familiarity with DB2 and other relational database software. Fourth-generation languages (4GLs) are less procedural and more like natural English, enabling their use for software development by managers and other users. Fifth generation languages (5GLs) include natural and intelligent languages, which are used for software development for artificial intelligence and expert systems.

There are over one thousand computer languages. It is essential that a programmer have a thorough knowledge of the language or languages in which programs are written in the organization where he or she seeks employment. Programmers must further possess a knowledge of general programming techniques and general relationships between program and hardware features. A strong orientation to detail is important in that something as small as a misplaced comma could cause system failure. This characteristic becomes crucial as a programmer *debugs* his or her programs to ensure they are error free. Debugging usually entails making trial runs on the computer with sample data.

Programs may be written in a matter of hours or may require more than a year of work. Thus programmers may work alone on small projects or in teams for larger projects. After completion of a program, the programmer must prepare an instruction sheet for the data-entry and computer operators who will enter the data into the computer and run the program. The work of these operators will be described in Chapter 4.

There are three types of programmers at work in most organizations: operating systems programmers, applications programmers, and maintenance programmers.

OPERATING SYSTEMS PROGRAMMING

The work of operating systems programmers is highly technical in nature and somewhat difficult for the layperson to understand. Basically, systems programming involves writing sets of instructions to make the programming of computers easier; for example, programs that schedule the computer to deal with many tasks simultaneously. These sets of instructions, called *operating systems,* control the operation of the entire computer system. They frequently become a permanent part of the computer's memory so that all of the components and related equipment perform in harmony with one another. This requires a good technical knowledge of the parts of the computer and how they operate.

Because of their knowledge of operating systems, systems programmers often help applications programmers debug their programs by identifying the point in the computer's cycle of operations where a program has gone wrong. Systems programmers might even be involved in developing new computer languages or adapting existing languages to specific needs.

Operating systems programmers are employed in a variety of work environments. In addition to any sizable organization using computers, there is demand for systems programmers for computer manufacturers, computer service organizations, and management consulting firms—all of which are discussed in later chapters. The decline in the demand for operating systems programmers with mainframe skills is largely attributed to the explosion in the use of personal computers and networks. Systems programmers with knowledge in telecommunications, database concepts, and expert and imaging systems will find many opportunities.

A degree in computer science with a solid background in computer architecture, which is the way the computer circuits are structured, is required for most positions. In addition, one year of Assembler language programming is desirable. A systems programmer might move upward, eventually becoming manager of programming, then move into systems analysis or database administration. Some systems programmers who enjoy technical rather than managerial activities may prefer to remain in programming.

APPLICATIONS PROGRAMMING

Applications programmers prepare computer program logic flowcharts according to specifications of the systems analyst. They write, debug, and test computer programs designed to solve an organizational problem or to fill an informational need. Not only does the programmer need knowledge of programming to be effective, but also a knowledge of the activities of the organization and the ability to communicate clearly with those involved outside the information processing department.

Applications programmers specialize in one of two major areas. The first is scientific, or engineering applications programming; the second is business, or commercial applications programming. The area of specialization is continued if the programmer moves into systems analysis.

Scientific Applications Programming

Scientific or engineering applications programming involves developing programs that solve scientific or engineering problems—in other words, applications that are mathematical in nature. There is an increasing demand for specialists in optical technology, artificial intelligence, and in all of the hot technology areas discussed in Chapter 1. Also valuable is exposure to the use and integration of personal computers into a larger system. Opportunities will depend in part on the level of federal spending and industry commitment in areas such as design automation, aerospace, graphics, numerical control, and quantitative methods.

The challenges are great in scientific programming. The intense investigation of the space shuttle disaster in 1986 revealed fatal design flaws requiring more than two-hundred modifications to the spacecraft. However, the shuttle's computer software was found to be of the highest quality: the implication is that error-free software for complex real-time systems in national defense, manned space flight, reactor control, and air traffic control is an achievable goal. IBM, the prime NASA contract developer, developed six on-board flight software systems consisting of about 500,000 lines of code with an error rate of .1 errors per thousand lines of code. The average industry rate is between 8 and 10 errors. While error-free software is possible, its cost is estimated at $1,000 per line of code, much too expensive for most applications. But the process used to develop such software provides programmers with insights into better software development.

An undergraduate degree in engineering, math, or the physical sciences is a minimum requirement. Some background in FORTRAN, Pascal, Assembler, or C programming languages is necessary. Also desirable are a master of science degree, large-scale and personal computer hardware exposure, and systems programming experience.

Business Applications Programming

Business or commercial applications programming involves a wide range of tasks, from developing programs to handle such routine business activities as billing customers to developing programs designed to satisfy the complex informational needs of managers. The improved quality and quantity of software packages in business applications has reduced the demand for applications programmers. However, every type of industry requires industry-specific software and many of the packaged software products fall short of meeting individual company needs. In this case, applications programmers must modify elements of the package and develop programs to integrate both new and existing software to best serve the company's purposes. There is a trend in some organizations to combine applications programming and systems functions into a single group. The myriad of new technologies, including CASE tools, has made both systems and applications programming decisions more complex.

Programming experience usually pays off in landing desirable jobs if it is pertinent to the systems in use in a company. New languages and CASE tools, dramatic shifts to decentralization of information systems functions, and the use of LANs have created many new opportunities in software development. Those in greatest demand will have had some exposure to job control languages, database systems, structured systems design, and distributed processing techniques.

The widespread use of personal computers has created a strong demand for programmers experienced in Pascal, visual C++, and visual BASIC on small commercial systems. Besides developing applications programs, personal computer programmers also support such functions as communications, graphics, database, or operating systems. With the demand for personal computers comes a demand for new and better software. Opportunities for personal computer programmers to work in the software industry will increase. The demand for programmers with knowledge of workstation technologies such as teleprocessing, word processing, electronic mail, and the integration of office automation and data processing functions is increasing. Also skills in two- and three-dimensional graphics and video games design and programming are rapidly increasing in demand. Computer graphics programmers have strong backgrounds in computer science since these programs are large and complex with many sophisticated algorithms, extensive databases, and careful user interfaces.

MAINTENANCE PROGRAMMING

Because of the enormous number of elements involved in most computer systems and the fact that most large programs are never completely debugged, there is a need for maintenance programmers. The maintenance programmer works constantly to enhance or repair the existing major programs. Since very little has been written on debugging techniques, substantial skill and experience in program development are required by the maintenance programmer. In addition, a very high level of analytic ability is needed. Some bugs result from correcting other bugs during maintenance, so the entire procedure can become quite complex. Because major computer programs interact in complex ways, both with systems software and hardware and at times with other programs, the definition of bug types and correction techniques is vital to keep things going. The maintenance programming staff usually consists of newly hired programmers and highly skilled veterans. In this way, the beginner can gain an overall familiarity with the systems in operation in the organization and can be trained by some of the most experienced programmers on the staff. In many settings several years of COBOL programming experience will prove useful in maintaining large systems with extensive programming in COBOL.

CAREER LEVELS IN PROGRAMMING

As with the systems analyst, there are various levels at which programmers might work in the course of their careers. Figures 3.1 and 3.2 show some of these levels for systems and applications programmers and their common position titles. Note that these are levels within a medium-sized organization

Figure 3.1   Systems Programming Career Path   **Figure 3.2   Applications Programming Career Path**

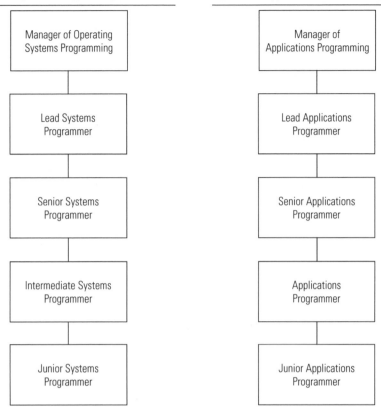

and will be fewer or greater in number and perhaps organized somewhat differently depending on the size of the organization. Advancement levels are comparable to those of the systems analyst in the degree of supervision and responsibility. Applications programming may be in either scientific or business applications, and maintenance programming will have a similar hierarchy to that of systems and application programming. The manager of operations systems programming is responsible for planning and directing the activities of the operating systems section and assigning personnel to projects. The senior systems programmer works independently at the highest technical level and may specialize in the support, maintenance, and use of one or more major operating systems. This position may involve directing those at lower levels. The intermediate systems programmer works under general supervision but may work independently on some tasks. At this level, the programmer may specialize in the support of one or a few operating system components or subsystems. The junior systems programmer usually has a good background in data processing and knows or is learning Assembler language. At this time, operating systems programmers are paid more than applications programmers at comparable levels because of their higher technical skills.

The manager of applications programming, like the manager of operating systems programming, is in full charge of the section; that is, he or she has overall responsibility for the development of effective and efficient programs. The lead applications programmer assists in planning, organizing, and controlling the section in an assistant manager capacity. The senior applications programmer works independently with program designs or specifications at the highest technical level, whereas the applications programmer and intermediate applications programmer usually work on only one or a few applications under general supervision. The junior applications programmer is often learning to program and works under direct supervision. More defined levels exist in applications programming because they comprise the largest number of programmers. Their numbers will continue to increase as will their salaries.

PROJECT TEAMS

Depending on the nature or size and scope of a programming project, the most effective way to get the job done might be through teamwork. Teams might include only programmers, or they might include programmers, systems analysts, technical writers, program librarians, and users who are subject matter specialists. Each team has a leader who has ultimate responsibility for the success of the project and for the supervision of team members. Although the team approach is being used more and more because of the magnitude of projects and extended computer services, it is not always popular with programmers. Past surveys of programmers revealed that as a group they have a low tendency toward social interaction on the job; that is, they exhibit a low need to work with other individuals. Whether or not the programmer or analyst is required to participate in team projects or the extent to which teamwork is used in an organization can be determined in the employment interview.

Software companies have complained that universities are not stressing large team projects nor exposing students to the latest tools or coding problems. But the universities counter with the argument that the tools change constantly; therefore university studies should be broader in scope. Programming teams, however, are here to stay. Some schools are involving seniors in large commercial projects proposed by companies. This preparation is very valuable in today's job market.

TECHNICAL WRITING

A factor creating a need for specialized technical writers is the increased emphasis on documentation. In order to implement a system and keep it operational, documents are needed to describe the system, the programs it comprises, the data input and its format, the informational output, changes made to the system, authorships, and other pertinent facts. These documents also include user manuals to show operators how to use the equipment, reference manuals for programmers, field service documentation to support hardware and software, marketing brochures, and other types of documentation needed to promote the system. In small- to medium-sized departments, documentation is done by the computer programmer. This is tremendously time-consuming, not to mention the fact that most programmers are not trained in writing. The answer to this dilemma is for computer manufacturers and large user organizations to employ skilled technical writers to document programs and systems. Documentation tends to be of higher quality when done by a writer who wants to write than by a programmer who doesn't.

As a profession, technical writing is coming into its own as demand for better documentation increases. No longer the low-paid stepchild of the computer team, the technical writer is more often participating throughout the entire project, beginning at the systems design and specification stage. What used to be a clerk-level salary is now competitive with salaries of the technical staff. Growth in the importance of technical writing can be attributed to several factors: the explosion in technology, the need for computer professionals and users to keep current, the efficiency of a synthesis of communication for those working with a system, and the need to provide a general understanding of the hardware and software. And all of this is cost-effective. The work of technical writers requires not only writing skills and documentation techniques, but verbal communications skills as well. Writers work directly with users to be sure that they understand the use of the system. In addition, technical knowledge of hardware, applications, and programming languages is required of technical writers. Those who want to work for companies marketing computer hardware, software, or services should have a background in various advertising techniques. Based on the premise that it is easier to teach technical subjects to a professional writer than to teach a technician to write, many companies employ writers with degrees in English and some technical background, or they provide company training. It is not unusual for an English teacher to switch to technical writing.

LIBRARIANS

After programs and documentation are produced, they are placed in the care of program and documentation librarians. The program librarian maintains the on-line and off-line libraries of programs. This requires programming skills. In addition, there may be a librarian responsible for the library of technical documentation, which includes descriptions of programs and how to run them. These two individuals ensure that users have all the information necessary to best use the system. The ability to organize materials and to retrieve them quickly for users is vital. As always, the size of the data processing department governs the number of librarians and how specialized their functions are.

TRENDS IN PROGRAMMING

According to recruiters in the software development industry in Canada, a shortage of about 4,000 software development professionals existed in 1994. Systems programmers to provide internal support for newly implemented database and telecommunications systems are in demand today as are network and client-server software specialists. These areas will be discussed in Chapter 5. New technology will affect the future outlook for applications programmers and change the nature of programming jobs. But some companies have not adopted the new technology very rapidly for a number of reasons. First, they have too much invested in the old languages. Extensive program libraries with programs written in COBOL, RPG, and Pascal guarantee maintenance programming jobs. Old programs, modified and enhanced, are being used along with new ones. Second, managers are uncertain as to what new methodologies to adopt, since change is expensive and newer, better developments continue to flood the market.

While program generators have existed for years, only CASE tools have achieved a measure of popularity. More complex than their forerunners, they are not only able to generate standard data entry and file update applications, but are also able to perform more sophisticated, complex tasks as well. However, a survey revealed that training time to master the use of CASE tools can range from sixty-nine to eighty-six hours. The tools in their current state can effectively reduce development time for simple projects, such as the automating of clerical tasks, but the longer, more complex the application, the less of a time savings with CASE tools. Findings showed that the tools shift the time expenditure to the front end of the development life cycle; that is, more time is spent in systems design and less is spent in coding. This reduces programming time but does not eliminate applications development jobs overall. Proponents feel that this is conducive to the development of better systems. Trends point to widespread decentralization of information systems using personal computers and LANs. Conversion specialists in both systems analysis and programming will be in great demand. Personal computer programmers will be in demand. Applications programmers may find additional opportunities in the software industry or as contract programmers since many companies today are *outsourcing*, the new buzz word for shifting their applications development activities from in-house to outside contractors. Those interested in programming careers should prepare themselves with these trends in mind.

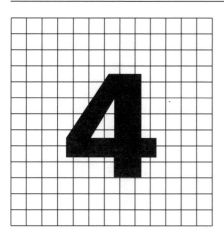

CAREERS IN OPERATIONS AND WORD PROCESSING

Automation of data centers is occurring in many companies today to increase efficiency, cut payroll costs, and reduce downtime. Automated console operations can reduce the amount of human intervention necessary to correct system errors. Leaders in automated operations are the finance, insurance, and utilities industries where downtime and errors are particularly costly. But still operations offers many and varied jobs. The operations personnel are the people who enter data and instructions into the computer (*input*), run the computer and its related machines (*peripheral equipment*), and retrieve the processed data (*output*). Entry into a number of operations positions requires very little training beyond high school, although little advancement beyond supervisory operations positions is possible without more formal education and training.

There is one special advantage to operations work. Since many organizations run their computers twenty-four hours a day, employees can work on flexible schedules. For example, a job in operations is ideal for a student who must work evenings. For the required level of education, the pay is good. Salaries will be discussed in a later section. While the systems development and programming personnel work primarily to produce software, the operations personnel are involved with the *hardware*, which is the computer itself and its related or peripheral equipment.

OPERATIONS

Although there are many openings in operations, the work of the computer professionals in this area is highly dependent on the state of technology, which rapidly changes. The innovations in computer hardware have impacted heavily on the nature of the specialized positions in operations. Operations personnel may have to learn to operate a new machine that replaces the one with which they are familiar. Flexibility is, therefore, important in operations jobs. The trend toward using personal computers and networks will have a large impact on the specialized jobs associated with the large computers. The keys to success and continued employment in operations are the development of transferable skills, a willingness to develop new skills that keep pace with technological change, and an eye to the future.

Jobs in operations vary quite a bit in function, yet movement from one section to another is common because of the limited training required for each position. Within the sections (computer operations, data entry, and production control) are various levels to which employees can advance as their careers develop. Supervisory positions are held by those who work up through the ranks. However, today those promoted to manager of operations usually have a good deal more formal education and experience than do most operations workers since these individuals must work closely with such highly trained individuals as the data communications managers, database administrators, managers of systems analysis, and managers of programming.

In charge of computer operations, data entry, and production control, the manager of operations must plan, direct, and control all computer and peripheral equipment operations, data entry, and production-control activities. In some centers, the manager also is responsible for operating systems programming, software maintenance, or applications maintenance programming. Because of the increased hardware and software complexity, the position is being continually upgraded. As the individual who provides the computer output to departments throughout the organization, the manager must have a broad knowledge of the company and be able to communicate with managers at all levels and across all departments. Minimum requirements for the position include supervisory operations experience and a good knowledge of installed hardware, software, and operating systems. In large installations, a college degree is required. As in every other area, a premium is placed on experience in network technology, telecommunications, and databases. The positions held by operations personnel are shown in Figure 4.1. As can be seen, the manager of operations has a number of different section managers or supervisors reporting to him or her. Remember that this structure may vary from one organization to another, but these positions do exist in most medium and large installations.

Computer Operations   The computer operations personnel are responsible for the general operation of the equipment including the central console, its on-line equipment, and its off-line (peripheral) equipment. This involves setting up the machine and mounting and removing the tapes, disks, and printer forms as required by the jobs being processed. Constantly monitoring the

Figure 4.1   Operations Career Path

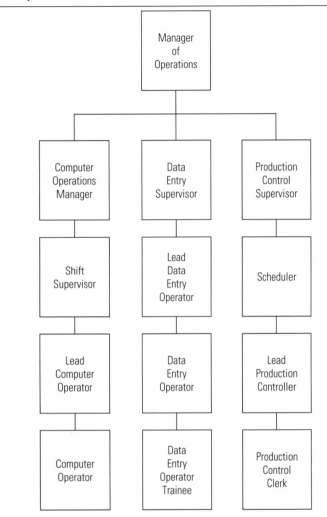

control panel, the operators adjust the equipment as directed by messages from the operating system and according to instructions in operations documentation. Troubleshooting if problems arise is a key part of the work. This is no small responsibility. Consider a modern nuclear power plant. A serious accident might cause one hundred alarms to go off with dozens of red lights flashing. The operator at the control panel must make some quick key decisions. Keeping a log of work completed also is required. Operators of modern, complex computer systems are trained to interact with the system to attain maximum efficiency from the hardware.

The manager of computer operations is responsible for the assignment of personnel to all activities involved in computer operations. Keeping the equipment "up," or operational, is a key function of the manager. The importance of the position is reflected in the fact that downtime could cost $200 per minute or more in medium to large installations. The value of the equipment itself is usually in the millions in large installations, and the manager is entrusted with control over the operation of it.

Assisting the manager is the shift supervisor, who may be responsible for the operation of large-scale computers during an eight-hour shift or the operation of a remote site. A lead computer operator may be responsible for all operations on a medium-sized computer or may operate the central console of a large machine. The computer operator assists the lead computer operator in running the computer and operates the central console in his or her absence. In smaller installations, the computer operator may operate the peripheral equipment as well. However, in larger installations, a peripheral-equipment operator performs this function, including setting up and operating tape drives, magnetic disk drives, printers, and off-line input/output equipment. The computer operator trainee always works under direct supervision in mounting tapes and disks, loading printers, or working on a peripheral subsystem. Librarians work closely with the operations staff in storing disks and tapes.

An alternative to advancing up the ranks in computer operations is going into programming, from which advancement into top management is possible. An operator may request programmer training but a college degree is often required for entry into and advancement in programming. Within the area of operations, a new position evolved from the increasing use of workstations and personal computers: the workstation or personal-computer manager. This manager is responsible for monitoring the use of personal computers that, through networks, are able to access the central computer and peripheral equipment throughout the company. Salaries of computer operators are good given the level of education required, and many individuals may be perfectly content to remain operators rather than take on the headaches of management. This is true in any data processing profession.

Data Entry

Data must first be prepared properly in order to be entered into the machine. Basic keyboard skills are required for this regardless of the method used (key-to-tape or key-to-disk). Data entry operators use terminals where data is typed onto a keyboard and displayed on a cathode ray tube (CRT) while being typed. Such terminals may be part of a self-contained personal computer or may be linked to a larger computer. These terminals have direct access to the central processor and are called *on-line systems*. Data and programs are entered on tape and disks and may be transferred to other devices, stored, and used over and over again. Those working in data entry may also perform a variety of clerical duties such as filing, typing, and answering the phone. Thus general office skills as well as speed and accuracy on the keyboard are required for the job. High school or vocational school offers training in these skills.

The data entry supervisor is responsible for the data entry staff and keeps things running efficiently. Distributing the workload among the data entry operators and monitoring the equipment to be sure it is working properly is part of the job. The lead data-entry operator may be responsible for an eight-hour shift or for one site in a multisite environment. Requiring only general supervision, the data entry operator is qualified to operate one or more data entry devices. Finally, the data entry trainee works under direct supervision in learning to operate the equipment.

As in the case of the computer operator, the data entry operator, without additional formal education, has advancement opportunities only up to the level of data entry supervisor. Depending on the individual, this may be satisfactory. If not, since operations run twenty-four hours in most installations, working out a schedule to allow for additional education is possible.

Production Control   Especially important in any size organization is the control of all equipment to ensure maximum production efficiency. The production control staff has the responsibility of evaluating jobs to be scheduled, arranging them in order of priority, and then determining what went wrong with jobs that did not run. While data entry is concerned with input, production control handles output, routing jobs to the proper place upon completion. The production control supervisor has responsibility over the entire production control process. The supervisor may set up and schedule jobs for processing or may delegate this to a scheduler. Like the lead computer or data entry operators, the lead production control clerk may have responsibility for production control over an eight-hour shift or over a single site in a multisite organization. Generally, the production control clerk prepares jobs for processing, enters the correct job commands, and gathers the output for routing. Under direct supervision, the production control trainee learns the production control function.

WORD PROCESSING

As one door closes to computer professionals, another invariably opens. Many of the small computer systems coming into use today are specifically "dedicated" to certain functions. Two such functions include computer-assisted design and computer-generated graphics. These special functions offer opportunities to those creative individuals with backgrounds in design or graphics who also have an interest in computers. An even more widespread use of dedicated small systems is in word processing. Word processing has become a field in itself with increasing job opportunities, education, and training programs.

Word processing arose from the need for more efficient and economical business communications. As the volume of paperwork required by businesses increased along with total office costs, including labor costs, the secretary's productivity tended to remain the same since the basic tools of the trade and the standard office activities remained unchanged. Then advancing technology enabled the development of word processing systems where activities are highly integrated to increase efficiency and lower costs.

Word processing uses a computer to prepare material that otherwise would have been written by hand or typed on a typewriter. The text is entered using a keyboard and CRT. A word processing program enables the text to be edited and rearranged with material inserted or deleted very quickly, without redoing the entire text, as is usually the case with typed manuscripts. High-speed laser printers produce as many copies of the text as wanted, each letter-perfect, in a fraction of the time it would take to produce the document on the typewriter. The text can be stored on disk or magnetic tape and changed as much and as often as desired.

Word processing is available on computer systems ranging in size from personal computers to large commercial installations. A keyboard, printer, CRT, and storage device for cassettes or disks are the tools for word processing. A standalone system includes these components with a personal computer. In a shared system, a terminal connected to the central computer and its peripherals is used. Computer vendors offer a variety of systems and software ideally suited to word processing functions.

A beginner with very little word processing experience holds the position of word processing trainee. Responsibilities include routine transcription and manipulation of text from various sources; for example, dictation, handwritten documents, and computer disks. The trainee also proofreads and keeps production records. Minimum requirements for the position are adequate typing skills, good grammar, the ability to use reference books, and willingness to work as part of a team. Those with six months to two years experience are promoted to the level of word processing operator. In this capacity, the operator handles special documents, meets quality standards, uses all of the machine's text-editing functions, and is familiar with department terminology and company practices. The word processing supervisor assigns work to the staff and monitors all activities to keep the center running as efficiently as possible. Training in word processing may be acquired in vocational schools and in some high schools as well.

Traditional clerical jobs have definitely been affected by the increased use of word processing. Although workers have been displaced, word processing technology has created new employment opportunities that more than compensate for the jobs eliminated—and this in the light of the perpetual shortage of clerical workers! Word processing was well-received by clerical workers from its inception. Early surveys showed that workers believed that word processing improved their positions as a whole and opened up more opportunities for advancement within their companies. On the negative side, office workers in organizations of all sizes complained about not being involved in the selection of equipment.

Health problems have afflicted some who hold jobs working with computer keyboards and other equipment. One of the most common problems is repetitive motion disorder, also called repetitive stress injury. Carpal tunnel syndrome is in this category; it affects the pathway for nerves that travel through the wrist. Symptoms begin with a burning or tingling sensation that gives way to loss of muscle strength, then numbness, and finally chronic pain. It is estimated that over a million people suffer from this. According to Bureau of Labor Statistics, repetitive stress injury is the most common and fastest growing work-related injury today. About 190,000 cases are reported each year. Medical professionals studying the problem have developed guidelines for using computer terminals, and there is pressure on organizations to adopt them. These guidelines call for proper position at the keyboard with stops every two hours to rest and stretch the back, shoulders, neck, and hands.

With word processing, the role of the private secretary has most often been upgraded to that of administrative assistant, and new supervisory and management positions have been created for clerical personnel within the word processing center. Since the work within the center is highly specialized and very routine, those individuals who prefer more of a variety of functions should seek employment in a smaller organization.

CAREERS IN TELECOMMUNICATIONS AND NETWORK TECHNOLOGY

Personal computer networking is one of the fastest growing niches in the computer industry. While a computer operating by itself is a useful tool, a computer network is what enables corporations to get the latest information as it happens and react to competitive and changing markets. Those *hubs* and *routers* that link PCs to networks and manage the information flow between them have given individuals access to company computer systems, vast databases, document files, and E–mail. In the future, multimedia computing and videoconferencing will become common applications. Information housed in massive databases and transmitted via networks is the driving force behind most large organizations. A profusion of networks already in existence have created opportunities for both businesses and individuals. Professionals experienced in network technology are in great demand. They play a vital role in keeping an organization current and competitive.

Telecommunications technology has had a tremendous impact on how both organizations and individuals receive and transmit large amounts of information today. The fiber optic infrastructure currently being put in place will create the information superhighway, a network capable of sending information a billion bits per second and faster. Using networks consisting of communications media and software to join two or more computer systems enables companies and individuals to access vast databases and transmit or receive information across the organization and the world.

TELECOMMUNICATIONS AND NETWORK PROFESSIONALS

Communications and network systems give managers and workers easy access to information within the company as well as to vast databases and information sources worldwide. These systems are designed to get the right information to the right person as rapidly as possible. Some organizations place such a value on this that they have invested millions of dollars in these systems. The complexity of these systems has given rise to problems of hardware and software selection, management, and security. Use of communications specialists and consulting firms are common as firms try to get the most from their investment.

The telecommunications group includes a manager and a number of specialists, depending on the size of the organization. Telecommunications involves the utilization of both hardware and software to link a computer to remote terminals or other computers. The telecommunications manager is responsible for the design of communications networks and the installation and operation of data links. Telecommunications analysts work under the manager. They must be knowledgeable in not only languages and applications, but in communications devices as well. They are responsible for program design, coding, testing, debugging, documentation, and implementation of telecommunications software. Their work also involves the evaluation and modification of existing communications hardware and software. They function as technical advisors to applications programmers.

If hired by a computer firm, a telecommunications specialist will work in a group developing new communications software. In the telecommunications industry, computer scientists and electrical and computer engineers are at work on network planning, software and information systems design, and research and development of new technologies. Positions in the computer and telecommunications industries will be discussed in detail in Chapter 6.

Advancements in network technology have introduced two new positions into the information field. The network engineer designs networks and transmission systems and conducts traffic studies. Network engineers may be employed in companies with large communications installations or in the telecommunications industry. The network administrator is responsible for the coordination and use of the local area networks (LANs) and wide area networks (WANs) throughout the organization. Network analysts do specific systems analysis under the administrator.

TECHNOLOGICAL TRENDS

Extensive use of the new technologies offer many opportunities for applications analysts and developers. Development of software and devices to implement and improve the use of communications and network technology will keep a lot of professionals busy.

- Voice mail involves voice storage and forwarding systems that enable users to leave, receive, and store verbal messages for people worldwide.
- Electronic mail (E–mail) enables a sender to connect to a system or network, enter a message, and send it to another person.

- Personal communications devices using wireless and conventional phone networks are smaller, lighter, and use less power than traditional cellular phones and offer pagers and messenger systems that can receive and store E–mail.
- Electronic document distribution involves transporting documents over communications lines and networks.
- Telecommuting enables employees to work at home using a personal computer or terminal linked to the office computer via a modem.
- Teleconferencing centers use voice, video, and audio systems to enable participants at distant locations to have a conference.
- Group-work software and technology allow people to share ideas, documents, and information around the office or the world.
- Electronic data interchange uses network systems that allow output from one system to be processed directly as input to other systems.
- Public network services such as CompuServe and Prodigy give personal computer users access to databases and services for an initial fee plus usage fees.
- Internet, which was originally for U.S. government defense work, is now used in over thirty countries by millions of individuals, organizations, and governments as a network of networks around the world. It is based on the World Wide Web (the Web) which is an expanding collection of documents that combine text, images, sound, and video.
- The information highway, also called the information superhighway or infobahn, is being developed to tie organizations, individuals, governmental agencies, and a variety of hardware, software, and telecommunications equipment together into one massive network.

The above applications are only a sample of the smorgasbord of offerings enabled by the continuing development of the new technologies. Computer and telecommunications specialists will play exciting roles in enhancing these and creating other applications in the future.

Data Security

Because of the value of information to an organization, it must be protected. The proliferation of personal computers and networks has intensified security problems. Increasing problems are occurring as networks offer easy access to information by outsiders. The director of security in an organization is responsible for information security throughout the entire organization. Theft, damage due to disasters such as fire or flooding, fraud, invasion of privacy, and a host of other problems plague organizations more and more as operations become decentralized and networks become common. More problems are caused by computer *viruses*, which are commands illegally entered into computer systems to alter or erase information, and illegal entry to data files by computer *hackers*, persons whose skills in breaking entry codes are witnessed frequently in real life (not just the movies). In addition, computer mistakes and accidents have become more frequent.

Computer security specialists are employed to protect data and computer resources. These positions require expertise in business, technology, and communications. In data security and disaster recovery, analysts must know what computerized functions a business cannot afford to lose. People working with data security tend to have programming and systems analysis backgrounds, since they are familiar with software. Hands-on experience goes a long way in this field. Those who have a technical industry specialty can command a higher salary. Disaster recovery personnel usually come from operations with telecommunications expertise. The director can come from either background. Data security involves not only work on the computer with the systems but a lot of communicating with people in the organization as well. Data security analysts may have had experience in auditing as well.

Many corporations hire outside companies or consultants to set up and/or evaluate their security systems. Tiger teams composed of computer security experts conduct raids on information centers to expose security loopholes. With the infusion of viruses into systems, major privacy problems as networks proliferate, and computer crime on the rise, security analysts speculate that the majority of large companies use such teams. Also hired are individual computer hackers who specialize in electronically attacking computer systems to be sure security systems work. Whether designed internally or externally, someone must constantly monitor the security system and report to top management.

The Auditor

The auditor, like the data security analyst, is concerned with security issues, but the auditor's job is much broader in scope. Involving every aspect of an organization's information systems, an audit is conducted to be sure that things are being done according to design. The auditing of computer services may be conducted by internal auditing personnel or by external auditors from professional accounting firms who report to the top-level information executive. The auditor must have a background in systems analysis or programming as well as accounting. Basically, the auditor inspects all programs, documentation, control techniques, the disaster plan, insurance protection, fire protection, and other systems aspects. *Auditing around the computer* is a method of examining the computer input and output to determine its accuracy. *Auditing through the computer* involves verifying the accuracy of the computer program through the use of test data to test processing accuracy and control procedures built into the program. A test program or an audit software package may be used to process the company's data. By comparing the results of the audit program and the company's own programs, the auditor is able to detect unauthorized changes in company programs that could reveal fraud. The auditor reports the findings of the evaluation to upper-level management, along with recommendations to insure system integrity and accuracy. AT&T Bell laboratories have developed a continuous-process auditing system that enables a business to audit its systems on a continuous basis.

Thus auditing is another type of computer career and another skill likely to stay in demand as computing services within organizations continue to increase. Exposure to different computer systems, programming languages, and application areas is highly desirable for auditors working for CPA firms. Senior programmers or analysts within an IS department may advance professionally into an auditing position. An average annual salary for auditors is $46,114. More emphasis in auditing is now being placed on database management and telecommunications. Most auditors hold a college degree—an MBA or CPA is desirable. In addition, excellent communications skills and a minimum of two years experience in the design and programming of business systems are usually expected. Many take the CISA exam to become Certified Information Systems Auditors.

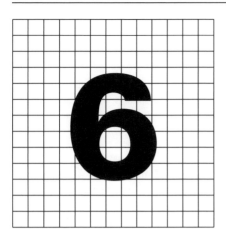

CAREERS IN THE COMPUTER INDUSTRY

Over the past five years the computer industry has been characterized by restructuring, dramatic growth in some sectors, downsizing in others, joint ventures, and, as always, fierce competition. The computer industry is composed of both established corporations and a constant flow of newcomers. Individuals considering careers in the industry are well advised to keep current by reading business and computer journals. Though computer professionals generally find better career opportunities inside the industry, its dynamic nature impacts job security. According to a 1995 *Fortune* magazine survey appearing in the March 6, 1995 issue, two of the ten most admired companies among all industries in America today are computer manufacturers Microsoft at number 2 and Hewlett–Packard at number 10. These companies were ranked according to the following criteria: quality of management, quality of product or services, financial soundness, value as a long-term investment, use of corporate assets, innovativeness, community or environmental responsibility, and ability to attract, develop, and keep talented people. The last criterion is particularly important to career planners.

The survey ranked companies within the computer industry in two segments as follows:

Computers and Office Equipment

Ranking	Company	Ranking	Company
1	Hewlett–Packard	6	Pitney Bowes
2	Compaq Computer	7	Seagate Technology
3	Sun Microsystems	8	Conner Peripherals
4	Apple Computer	9	Unisys
5	IBM	10	Digital Equipment

Computer and Data Services

Ranking	Company	Ranking	Company
1	Microsoft	6	First Data
2	Oracle Systems	7	Computer Sciences
3	Electronic Data Systems	8	Computer Associates International
4	Automatic Data Processing	9	Dun & Bradstreet
5	First Financial Management	10	Comdisco

The large computer companies manufacture and market both hardware and software. For years software development lagged behind. As more improved and less expensive hardware continued to be manufactured, a gap grew between the development of more powerful and versatile hardware and the development of software enabling the advanced systems to be used to their full potential. To fill this gap, the software industry emerged—led by such companies as Microsoft, Lotus Development, and Borland International. The software industry is the most dynamic in information technology and is where dramatic growth will occur in the future. Companies start up, fail, merge, acquire other companies, and introduce new products every year. The outsourcing trend will contribute greatly to the growth of the data services industry.

Job seekers should do some in-depth industry research to help in their job searches. It would be wise to see how companies rank in revenues and growth in specific areas, such as mainframes, personal computers, data communications, data services, peripherals, software, and so on, depending on the segment of interest of the individual. Stock market data are helpful in finding growing companies, particularly when an individual is considering employment with a smaller firm. As do other industries, the computer industry fluctuates with the business cycle. When seeking employment it is important to consider both the industry as a whole and the patterns of growth, revenues, employment, and employee compensation and benefits of individual firms.

User groups are taking an influential role in vendor product development and enhancement. These groups, the ultimate consumers, help shape vendor policy and direct emphasis. In information systems the emphasis has changed from hardware to software. Industry segments grow at different rates. Growth in the areas of personal computers and telecommunications equipment has been and will continue to be very strong. While mainframes remain at the heart of some large systems and supercomputers have been introduced, the power packed into personal computers and networks make them the focal point of the industry. As computer expert U.S. Navy Captain Grace M. Hopper, special advisor in the Naval Data Automation Command, once put it, "Just remember, it wasn't the dinosaurs who survived; it was the lizards."

Careers within the computer industry can be grouped into four areas: design, manufacturing, sales, and services. These areas afford a variety of jobs for computer professionals. Within these areas an individual may work with a specific major product line. Since the larger computer companies offer a wide array of products, a computer professional may choose to specialize in equipment designed for use within certain areas, such as networks and telecommunications, multimedia systems, expert systems, imaging technology, or certain industry segments such as education, manufacturing, business, laboratories, engineering, and so on.

COMPUTER DESIGN

Computer professionals are employed by the computer industry in the areas of both hardware and software engineering. Key areas of specialization today include communications networks, workstations, optoelectronics, supercomputers, factory automation, multimedia systems, and expert systems.

Hardware Engineering   Since computers are primarily electronic machines, computer engineers require strong backgrounds in electronics. These engineers are, therefore, electrical and electronics engineers who specialize in the design of computer systems. They are hired by computer manufacturers to design the central processor and peripheral equipment such as terminals, printers, and tape and disk drives. A tremendous number of opportunities for electrical engineers exist today; in fact, they are at the top of the most-wanted list for all occupational groups. This is due to the explosive growth in high-technology areas. Electrical engineers undergo a good deal of vigorous, formal education. An undergraduate degree—and for some positions a graduate degree—in engineering is required. Most engineering jobs in the computer hardware industry offer a high degree of security and the opportunity to transfer skills from job to job.

Advancement from associate engineer to the positions of senior and principal engineer and also into management is possible. Some engineers who have the formal education and a good amount of experience choose to go out on their own as engineering consultants. Electrical engineers work in the areas of production and maintenance as well as design. Some companies will have the engineer who plans the project retain responsibility for carrying it through to completion.

Other engineers involved in the design process are mechanical and metallurgical engineers. These engineers design the mechanical parts making up the computer's structure—the housing for all computer parts—and develop new conductive and resistive materials for use in computer circuits. Computer facilities planners make mechanical and electrical drawings, plan hardware layouts, do capacity configuration, and calculate electrical requirements to prepare a site for a chosen computer. Positions in telecommunications design require a B.S. in engineering. These highly trained people are very much in demand and are paid very well.

Scientists in chemistry and physics are also involved in computer hardware design and work closely with the engineers. In addition, computer technicians are employed to assist the scientists and engineers. They hold a variety of jobs. Drafters and engineering aides make drawings, complete calculations, and check specifications of plans developed by the engineers. The requirement for entry into a computer technician job is a high school education with a good background in math and science or a two-year technical degree in drafting, electronics, or a related area. Computer technicians also are employed in the manufacture and maintenance of computer hardware.

Software Engineering

Software engineering has had difficulty keeping pace with the fast changing and rapidly growing capabilities of computer hardware. Thus, there is a tremendous demand for software engineers to produce the sophisticated programs, languages, and operating systems required to fully utilize these advanced capabilities. While these software engineers are basically analysts and programmers, the position title of programmer is rarely used within the computer industry itself. Software engineers work in the following areas: developing new computer languages, operating systems, and applications packages; systems analysis and development; diagnostics and reliability testing; research; and simulation. The detailed work of systems analysts and programmers has already been discussed in previous chapters.

Since software engineers work on the cutting edge of the new technology, they must have excellent skills. Most hold degrees in computer science or mathematics with strong analysis and programming backgrounds. However, a liberal arts degree holder with substantial computer and programming experience is strongly considered for a software engineer position, especially to work in the development of expert systems.

COMPUTER MANUFACTURING

To manufacture computers, a company requires many individuals with different educational backgrounds to perform a variety of tasks. A key position is that of the manufacturing engineer, who usually holds a degree in mechanical, electrical, or industrial engineering. This individual oversees the entire production process, including the efficient use of materials, machines, and labor. Detailed planning of the location of machines, the movement of tools or parts, and the order of operations is the responsibility of the manufacturing engineer. A number of universities throughout the country now offer degrees in manufacturing engineering, or offer it as an option within industrial or mechanical engineering. Also available are two- and four-year degrees in manufacturing engineering technology, which are less theoretical programs with more hands-on experience. The trend is toward increased formal education. Even the value of apprenticeship programs will diminish in the years ahead.

Manufacturing engineers are employed in all industries, but opportunities abound in the computer industry. In addition, computer technology is greatly impacting the design and construction of new factories. Automation and robotics are now common in most manufacturing environments. In other words, knowledge of computer technology is valuable to manufacturing engineers working outside the computer industry as well as those working within it.

Assisting the manufacturing engineer is the manufacturing technician, who prepares specific detailed plans based on the general ideas of the engineer and communicates them to the assemblers and inspectors. Generally, the technician holds an associate degree from a junior or community college.

There is a great demand for assemblers and inspectors in computer manufacturing. These jobs are typical of jobs in electronics manufacturing in that they involve precise stamping, cutting, soldering, and wiring along with thorough testing of circuits and switches. Inspectors check and double-check the work in progress. One small oversight or a bit of sloppiness could have disastrous results. Some jobs in assembly and inspection require formal training in electronic circuitry, but most workers develop their skills through on-the-job training. Assemblers and inspectors may work in factories in which components are both manufactured and assembled, or they may work in factories that produce specialized components.

The semiconductor industry supplies the completed tiny chips and circuit boards to the manufacturers. This special branch of the computer manufacturing industry requires specialized technicians. Photographic technicians photograph and make prints of circuit designs on boards, while chemical technicians etch pathways on the printed circuit boards onto which microchips are then mounted.

Along with the computer professionals discussed in this section, a host of other people who have backgrounds in general areas such as production, materials management, and quality control are employed in the manufacture of computers. Examples of the types of positions available are materials planner, buyer, production supervisor, product control planner, and quality control supervisor. They are held by those with degrees or experience in their specific areas.

SALES AND MARKETING

The key to selling computers, assuming there is a good product to sell, is marketing. Sales and marketing teams composed of personnel from hardware, software, systems development, consulting, documentation, market research, advertising, trade shows and exhibits, and sales administration and training combine their talents to market and sell their products. These professionals usually specialize by product line, such as mainframes, personal computers, or special purpose systems.

Sales Representatives   Sales or marketing representatives are the customer contact people. Typically, a sales representative calls on established accounts, makes presentations to prospective customers, works with field engineers, helps formulate marketing strategies, and assists in training new sales reps. As a sales or marketing trainee, the sales representative usually goes through a series of company-conducted courses to get a solid background in computer technology and company products. Then, working closely on the job with experienced sales reps and support staff, the trainee acquires the skills and knowledge needed to sell the products. The training program is usually rigorous, and everyone who sells the company's products goes through it regardless of former experience. Continuing-education opportunities both inside and outside the company are always available to sales reps.

Usually required for sales representative jobs are business or technical degrees coupled with a knowledge of computers and computer applications. Sales and marketing experience and knowledge also are very valuable. The sales representative may advance to the position of marketing manager. In this capacity the individual has responsibility for directing and evaluating the activities of the marketing representatives, but he or she may still have marketing duties with key accounts. Advancement from district-level management to regional and divisional levels and finally to group headquarters describes a possible career path. Management positions at these levels also might lead to more general management areas such as corporate product management. But an individual first must be effective in sales.

Sales careers have certain characteristics that might help one determine whether to opt for them. In general, sales reps help customer organizations find solutions to problems of managing their information resources. This involves exposure to many different types of people, businesses, and markets. Good communications skills are essential. A sales rep works independently with no direct supervision and can exercise a great deal of freedom in determining how to best get the job done. The computer market is a highly competitive and rapidly changing one. The sales rep is continually involved in keeping current on the state of technology and the competition. Compensation is based on sales, which is fine when sales are good, yet take-home pay varies from one month to the next. Needless to say, sales is not for everyone. But the independent, self-motivated, highly energetic, and fairly personable individual might find it a very gratifying career. Many choose to stay in sales rather than move into management. Sometimes salaries are higher in sales than in management—and without the headaches.

The computer industry is one of the most innovative in terms of use of personnel. For example, in 1993 Compaq Computer Corp. shifted its U.S. sales force into home offices equipped with computers, printers, fax/copiers, cellular phones, two phone lines, desk bookshelves, and credenzas. A sales rep can plug into Compaq's database from any phone jack or from a cellular modem. After a few sales calls, a rep returns home to write letters, respond to E–mail, fax clients technical reports, and update the common database with news about ongoing accounts. These sales reps occasionally check in at headquarters. Compaq set up a toll-free number for customers with routine inquiries about products, pricing, and availability, thus enabling sales reps to concentrate on developing and servicing accounts.

Marketing Support Personnel

As mentioned earlier, sales result from a team effort. Some specialists who support the sales force are described below. Marketing support specialists assist sales personnel in the technical aspects of sales presentations and provide guidance on systems installation. In-depth studies are conducted by systems analysts to determine how to install the system most efficiently. Applications analysts and software engineers develop software for use specifically with company equipment. Manuals are developed by documentation writers to acquaint users with the system and its use. Demand in the area of marketing support is increasing rapidly as the number of products in the marketplace increases. Technical expertise in such areas as database management systems, personal computer systems, visual display units, specialty software, and custom systems is highly desirable. The ability to relate new product specifications to customer needs is essential. Advancement into marketing management, technical services management, or consulting is possible.

COMPUTER SERVICE

Computer companies offer a variety of services to their customers. The quality of these services is critical to business. More emphasis is being placed on the importance of service workers and their productivity. In a Hewlett–Packard service center where employees answer phone calls from customers, a team of workers were allowed to choose their own supervisor. The areas in which service is offered include field services, software services, and educational services.

Maintenance

Field service representatives, also called field or customer engineers, perform a variety of tasks for the company. They are trained electronics technicians who install, make routine adjustments, diagnose problems, repair, and make modifications to systems. Field engineers are responsible for preventative and corrective maintenance of the equipment. Minimizing "downtime" once a customer's system is installed is a critical part of their job—since, as you recall, downtime is very expensive. Working directly with customers requires interpersonal skills as well as the technical skills required to solve tricky problems. In-house field engineers assist sales and support personnel in preparing the engineering portion of sales presentations to customers. They work directly with hardware and software design groups and with manufacturing and engineering staff to test, troubleshoot, and debug equipment and software. Field service representatives have at least two years of technical training, and some hold engineering or computer science degrees. Levels of experience include junior field service rep with little experience, associate field service rep with one to three years experience, field service rep with three to six years experience, and senior field service rep with more than five years of experience. Promotion to field service manager or supervisor involves the responsibility for overseeing a staff of field engineers.

Software Services   Technical support representatives help customers get the most from their equipment through installation of newly purchased software, training in its use, application consultation, diagnosis and resolution of software problems, and explanation of documentation. Such consulting services as systems analysis, running on-site workshops, conducting feasibility studies, modifying standard software, assisting with project management, and developing applications and systems programs are provided by technical support representatives. This area has been criticized by user groups. As computer and software systems become more numerous and companies buy equipment from various vendors which they integrate into their operations, the need for technical support increases. It becomes harder and harder to meet this need.

Vendors have found a way to use technology to give technical support to personal computer hardware and software. More are offering electronic bulletin board systems (BBSes) to give on-line support. These systems provide answers to the most commonly asked technical questions as well as access to other users who provide information as well. Independent subscription services such as CompuServe, Genie, and The Source provide special interest groups with information on specific products. These services are often monitored by the vendor's own technical support representatives.

In-house activities of technical support representatives include assisting the sales force by running seminars, giving technical presentations, assisting in the preparation of proposals, producing sales leads, and evaluating customer applications. Training for new personnel is given by the experienced specialists. Those desiring work in this area should have extensive software experience.

Educational Services   Large computer companies usually offer a wide range of courses to both employees and customers. In-house, the educational services specialists work with field service, software service, sales/marketing, management, or any group requiring training ranging from the most fundamental to the most complex topics. Comprehensive, state-of-the-art education in the areas of service, support, and utilization of company products is provided. Educational services teaches customers how to use the products they have purchased. Using literature and workbooks, laboratory facilities, videotapes, videocassettes, audio-synchronized filmstrips, and state-of-the-art computer systems, instructors develop and offer effective courses. Individuals with degrees in education and experience with computers or basic electronics, or with degrees in computer science and experience in teaching, can combine both interests in the area of educational services.

THE DATA SERVICES INDUSTRY

An industry unto itself is data services. There is a trend toward outsourcing in which a company hires another company to do some or all of its data processing.

Some companies continue to develop and maintain their own applications while running them remotely in the computer vendor's data center. For example, Eastman Kodak and NASA have outsourcing agreements with IBM. Many computer vendors provide information services in addition to their product lines. With substantial computer industry revenues in services, most major computer vendors offer services as well as products. Some companies specialize in and provide only data services. They process data for customers who neither own nor lease computers or for those requiring capacity in addition to that provided by their own computer. These organizations employ systems analysts, software engineers, operators, and sales and service representatives to perform those same tasks described in previous chapters.

Services offered include not only data processing but such professional services as systems review, systems planning, the entire systems analysis and design cycle, implementation of systems, documentation, and employee training. Specialization in certain industry applications is now being done in services organizations. For many customers these organizations provide a viable alternative to grappling with such problems as acquiring state-of-the-art equipment and hiring experienced systems analysts in a changing technological environment. They reduce uncertainty by providing a finished project on a set deadline. Professional services organizations, as they are often called because of the expanded services they now offer, afford yet another employment alternative for computer professionals.

Computer leasing enables companies to protect against obsolescence and avoid the cost of buying and maintaining equipment. Although leasing equipment is expensive as well, some companies feel that leasing makes more financial sense. Computer vendors offer attractive leasing arrangements with a provision for upgrading the leased equipment.

Another option open to companies is hiring a turnkey contractor. The duties of the contractor are the purchase, testing, and installation of hardware and software on the company's premises. This might involve dealing with several vendors to acquire what is needed for the system. The contractor may develop the required software or arrange for an independent contract programmer to produce it. Usually, large computer manufacturers have divisions designated as turnkey divisions.

THE SOFTWARE INDUSTRY

The software industry will experience remarkable growth with steady demand for new products. New operating systems and more complex application requirements will keep software designers very busy. Smaller yet ever more powerful computers will create much of this demand. The wider usage of networks establishes demand for more integration software. The technology in demand today is object-oriented design and programming. Expertise with popular languages such as C++ with Windows options is a requisite skill for professionals entering the software engineering field.

A hot area in software engineering is multimedia software such as CD–ROM-based encyclopedias, which use text, graphics, still and moving images, sound, speech, and music. Multimedia software will be widely used in education and entertainment and has applications in business areas as well. The next generation of multimedia will offer artificial or virtual reality, also called *cyberspace*, accessible to an increasing number of cyberpunks. This technology creates a computer-simulated environment that is interactive—such as the one in the film *Disclosure*. For scientific applications, visualization software uses large amounts of 3D data to generate many types of visual images. This enables the representative of complex scientific and advanced 3D design problems that occur in engineering, medicine, and other scientific fields. Software will be required for the new neural-network computers modeled after the way the brain works. Image-management software allows the compression and decompression of files for efficient and space-saving storage and retrieval.

Both large and small companies in the software industry will vie for the huge software market for years to come. Many companies are built around one main product. Newcomers can effectively compete with established companies. Career opportunities exist for those who can get in on the ground floor of a young growing company. However, the industry is volatile and companies do sometimes fail. But software expertise is easily marketable these days.

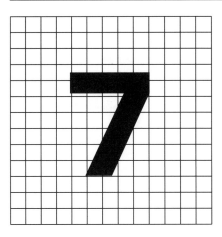

CAREERS IN INFORMATION SYSTEMS MANAGEMENT

Managing information resources involves all of the various components we have discussed including hardware, software, people, databases, telecommunications systems, and procedures used with an organization's information systems. It is far more complicated to discuss information systems (IS) management than it is to discuss other areas of management. The interrelationships between the various components in the field are complex and changing. The value placed on information has dramatically increased over the past decade. A recent *Computerworld* survey reported that roughly 64 percent of the companies involved had installed a system for competitive advantage during the last year. New information systems often cause major organizational changes including the roles people play in the company and their reporting relationships. Top-level information positions exist in most corporate structures; however, the responsibilities, power, and opportunities for advancement for information professionals within that structure are somewhat ambiguous because of the constant state of technological flux and the resulting dynamic structure of the modern organization.

According to a 1994 survey by Management Recruiters International, middle-level management positions are declining. New nonmanagement titles such as technical specialist and project leader have grown considerably. Reengineering has brought fundamental changes in how organizations view information systems careers. A decentralization of IS functions has resulted from the increasing use of personal computers and networks. The trend toward the outsourcing of IS activities has both eliminated jobs and reduced management responsibilities. The assignment of IS professionals to independent business units, in which they report to business managers rather than functional managers in systems development, has reduced the power of IS managers. And finally, the risk of making poor choices of technology in an environment of technological change threatens the very job security of IS managers. Many IS managers today are carefully evaluating their career paths. Those working outside the computer industry are weighing pros and cons of remaining or seeking employment with a computer vendor.

Demand is great for top-level managers with expertise in database management and telecommunications. Global information resource management is becoming very important as more organizations begin doing business in other countries. Advances in telecommunications and networks have given rise to effective global information systems. Experience in these will become significant in the future. Some of the responsibilities of line managers, such as managers of systems analysis, programming, and operations, have been described in previous chapters. This chapter will focus on information systems management jobs and the complexity of these jobs in relationship to the rest of the corporation.

THE EVOLUTION OF INFORMATION SERVICES

Back in the dark ages (less than a decade ago), computers were located in data processing departments. Early data processing was used in most organizations primarily for mundane business tasks, such as payroll and inventory applications. Managers of data processing had very little power within the corporate structure. They were viewed as highly technical specialists with little understanding of the organization and its activities other than basic accounting tasks. The data processing manager was far more comfortable with his assemblers and compilers than with corporate strategic planning.

The data processing department was remote from the rest of the organization, with a culture and a language all its own. Those outside the data processing department, including top management, felt uncomfortable with the language and somewhat intimidated by the machines. Communication was thus limited. The lack of knowledge of computers and their potential by top management and the inability of the data processing manager to communicate this potential to executives in language they could understand resulted in a failure to use the computer beyond the simplest applications. The lack of understanding of the organization and its functions by data processing managers reinforced top management's view of them as purely technocrats. Promotion to a line management position, from which advancement to executive levels was possible, simply did not occur. Thus the position of data processing manager was a dead-end job. It is no wonder that many programmers and systems analysts preferred to stay with their computers rather than assume the headaches of the data processing manager. Often these technically-oriented people lacked management and communication skills and infinitely preferred working alone.

The frustrations experienced by the data processing manager were numerous in that corporate decisions affecting the data processing department were made without involving him or her at all. On the other hand, since top management had little or no knowledge of computers, the data processing manager had total control over the purchase of hardware and software, and this did not always result in the best business decisions.

Though this situation may still exist in some small companies, most organizations realized that the computer could be used in more valuable ways than for simple business applications. The profusion of new packaged software for applications in virtually every industry, and the development of less expensive, more powerful computers changed the very nature of data processing. The field of management information systems was born. The computer could provide information for managerial decision making to managers of all levels in the organization. As managers used this information and began to realize its value for the first time, attitudes toward the entire information profession started changing. Advances in technology included more and more sophisticated software developed for managerial decision making. The widespread use of the personal computer, the executive's best friend, has also contributed to changing attitudes. The newer, younger executives are knowledgeable and proficient in the use of computers. The position of IS manager was developed and elevated beyond the level of the manager of the data processing department. Helping to identify the informational needs of managers throughout the organization and providing this information via the data processing department became crucial functions. Thus the term information processing displaced the term data processing in many organizations. Finally, the position of chief information officer (CIO) was created.

While information technology is acknowledged as vital to corporate growth and profitability, not all organizations have a CIO at the top management level and, in those that do, the influence of the CIO varies. Each organization has its goals and a organizational structure designed to meet those goals. The job of an IS manager is dependent on how information and technology are used to achieve company goals. In some companies technology and technologists are integral to the business. They are perceived as those capital assets that can give the company the competitive edge. Since technology is everybody's concern, there are no barriers between technical and nontechnical workers. In such companies the CIO plays a key role. Other companies regard IS as a cost rather than an asset and do not know how to best use information resources. In today's economy the role of the CIO may involve financing decisions regarding leasing and outsourcing, contractual negotiations with vendors and suppliers, and employee relations, including global staffing, customer service, and planning.

A recent phenomenon is that of the temporary chief information officer. With the use of outsourcing and the reduction of permanent IS personnel, some companies feel that they do not need a permanent senior level IS manager. They are hiring temporary CIOs who stay only long enough to reorganize the department, manage a specific project, or put a new system in place. These individuals are often recently-retired CIOs who command prorated salaries comparable to what a permanent CIO's salary would be.

THE JOB OF INFORMATION SYSTEMS MANAGER

IS is an immature discipline. Its corporate role is still evolving. More and more, IS managers are required to focus less on systems and more on services. This is reflected in a more frequently appearing job title: manager of information services.

The burden of communication is on the information professionals. They must reduce the amount of technical jargon used in discussing their services to company users. The information professional needs to know what functions are going on throughout the organization far more than a user needs to know technical aspects of information. The elite position previously held by the information professional speaking "computerese" has turned into a dead-end position held by an individual who lacks both the communications skills necessary to speak to users in language they can understand and the business skills required to know what users need. As user groups begin to make more of the decisions, both business knowledge and flexibility will be needed by IS professionals.

There are ways in which information managers create atmospheres within their organizations very favorable to their departments. One way is by holding user meetings to report on new developments in technology, how other organizations use them, and how they will be used in their organization. In addition, user needs are discussed and incorporated into the budgeting process. Another way to improve communications is via an information department newsletter. Technology fairs, in which vendors come into the company to display their products and services, greatly stimulate interest in the types of information services that are and could be available through the information department. As more analysts become part of business units, the composition of the systems development department will change along with the role of the information manager. Members of the department might also be assigned to projects on a permanent or temporary basis. A manager must be sensitive to the organic nature of an organization's structure and be flexible enough to adapt as the company adjusts its structure to changes in technology, competition, and business conditions. Since there is major emphasis in corporations on strategic planning, the understanding by IS managers of the strategic planning process is essential. Their ability to provide top-notch information relative to the process will affect their positions within the company.

ADVANCEMENT TO THE TOP

Those individuals who ultimately move into the position of CIO come from a variety of backgrounds, including engineering; physical sciences; business, particularly finance and management information systems; and computer science. Thus educational background is far less important than how one's career develops over time. Classically, those who become the key information executives have been with their companies over twenty years and have moved up through the ranks. Today, because of the expansion of information

Figure 7.1 Career Path to Top Management

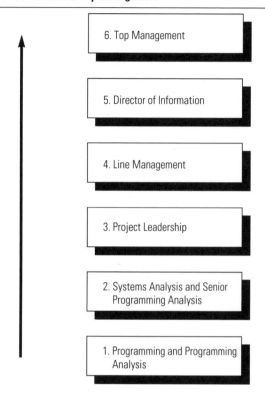

6. Top Management

5. Director of Information

4. Line Management

3. Project Leadership

2. Systems Analysis and Senior Programming Analysis

1. Programming and Programming Analysis

services and the creation of new management positions at higher levels, the time period is likely to be shorter. Still, in most cases, the information executive has been with the company for awhile and moved up through the ranks. This is not to say that earlier in their careers some of these individuals did not work for a number of different firms. Turnover in information management is legend, but the fact remains that the majority of information executives served a stint in their companies before being moved into the key position. It is important to plan one's career path and choose a company with this thought in mind. Figure 7.1 shows levels of IS management within a company.

Some observations on what is required for success have been made by those who are most successful in the industry. Characteristics such as decision-making skills, ability to explain things in simple language, and an understanding of business and the management style of the company are always included. Many things—such as intuition about people and the ability to work well with them—are developed in such complex ways that they cannot be built into an educational program. However, being personable and able to handle issues calmly and in a straightforward manner are behaviors people can develop.

Everyone does not aspire to top management. There is room at the top for only a few. If a manager of an IS department runs a shop of which he or she is proud and enjoys the job, why perceive it as dead-end? It is only dead-end if the manager believes he or she has the ability to go higher but is prevented by the organizational structure or organizational attitudes from advancing any further. Management at any level is not for everyone. Managerial skills are quite different from technical skills. The individual who loves the technical aspects of the job and disdains management is wise to remain in programming or systems analysis, develop technical expertise, and strive for promotion to senior consultant. A dilemma exists for all who are in scientifically- or technically-oriented professions. Do they gain managerial skills, move into management, and at each level have less and less involvement in the scientific or technical area that they have chosen and enjoy? Or do they remain scientists and technicians and leave the management to someone else?

Higher salaries, the desire to have an impact on the larger organizational issues, and a sense of advancement often attract people to management positions. At some point in an individual's career a choice must be made. Ideally, a programmer or analyst will have this choice. Some highly skilled programmers and analysts find themselves at a dead end because they are too hard to replace if moved into management. If management is their ambition, then they are forced to issue an ultimatum or to change companies.

Once promoted or committed to management, managers at any level should broaden their knowledge of networks, computer security, databases, telecommunications, and other areas to ensure their value to the company at higher levels. Because of the pressure to learn more about business, programmers and analysts have been entering Executive Master of Business Administration (EMBA) programs. These programs are designed for mid-career professionals who want a better business background but do not want to interrupt their careers to get it. Admission to such programs usually requires about ten years of working experience and some managerial responsibility. These programs stress on-the-job applications with a business orientation. The work and pressures are great, but then this, too, is excellent preparation for promotion to top-level management.

RESPONSIBILITIES OF MANAGERS

Corporate-level information managers, like all top-level managers, focus on strategic planning to achieve corporate goals and objectives. Determining the informational needs throughout the organization and the resources required to meet these needs is one major responsibility. Monitoring and reporting the status of all information operations to senior management is another. The position of vice-president of information or CIO is a recently created one in which the information executive participates at the highest level of the organization. Individuals to fill this position are very much in demand. Prior to the creation of this position, the director of MIS held the top-ranking information management position. This is still the case in many organizations. While this individual may not hold the rank or power of a corporate vice-president, the MIS manager has authority over all information operations and reports directly to top management. As IS management roles evolve, other key managers have or will assume authority over specific information areas.

Many managerial jobs are global in nature: budgeting for the entire department, conferring with managers from other areas, establishing the department and its services within the company, and so on. Thus the classic dilemma arises. How does a manager with so many responsibilities stay on top of the constantly changing technological scene? It is essential that the manager remain abreast of significant new developments in equipment and software, since it is he or she who will recommend these items for purchase and communicate their capabilities to key people. At the same time, the manager, who has been very technically adept, may lack knowledge of the business activities of the firm as well as crucial management skills. This knowledge and these skills must somehow be acquired. How can the manager juggle so many balls in the air?

As if the IS manager hasn't problems enough, the manager serves as a constant buffer between subordinates and those outside the department. Many highly technical individuals are loners, attracted to the job because they prefer working with data and machines rather than people. More and more these individuals must work closely with user groups and satisfy *their* needs. Although these users may lack technical know-how, they know what information they need to perform their jobs. To work in this new user-oriented environment, IS professionals need both communication skills and knowledge of business functions, neither of which is included in the usual computer science program.

Those who aspire to management levels should endeavor to learn something about management and the activities of the company even as starting programmers. In addition to preparation for management, they will be better prepared for integration into a business unit if organizational change requires such a move. Many middle-level management positions have decreased because of the need to cut costs, to hire practitioners familiar with the new technology, and to create positions for staff who will work directly with business users. The distinction between management and technical tracks is becoming very fuzzy. High-level technical specialists are earning as much as or more than managers. Patterns of influence and leadership are changing in information systems. Teams and peer-based evaluation and reward systems are being more widely used.

PROJECT MANAGEMENT

The changed nature of work is reflected in careers today. Middle managers have been reengineered right out of jobs. Computers now collect, analyze, and disseminate the information more efficiently and faster than humans ever did. Work is organized around projects that are conceived, staffed, completed, and shut down. These are replaced by other projects. Colleagues may be relative strangers with different areas of expertise. Most organizations have numerous ongoing projects. These projects are sometimes prioritized by an information-systems steering committee composed of senior management. Teams are developed to handle these projects headed by a project manager. Project management has certain advantages over other systems management jobs. It is easier to build cohesion and keep morale high in a smaller group that focuses on a specific project than in a whole department that deals with many. Project management provides excellent experience for the manager on the way up in that some of the small group strategies can work even in a larger group.

Those working on a project are part of a team. Team managers do not use the command and control strategy that other managers might. The role of the team manager is communication, conflict resolution, and coaching. An effective leader uses instinct and patience. The astute project manager usually has the team tackle a lot of the management headaches such as productivity. Use of such techniques as quality circles, nominal group technique, and consensus management can help in this. The team members, then, are able to develop some of the leadership skills needed to move into management. The manager, if the experience is positive, is more disposed to using participative management techniques in future positions, having lessened the fear of loss of control. This fear is experienced by managers at all levels. The project manager stands to learn a lot from the high level of technical expertise of the team members. In addition, if the project is a highly visible one, the manager stands to make points with top management. Project management is not without its problems, but it is a good position from which to advance, to update technical knowledge, and to gain some leadership skills for both the project manager and team members alike. Those who staff winning projects are in line for the next hot project. It is not organizational level that determines position and status but rather what successful projects an individual has played a vital role in.

OUTSOURCING

A major trend that has caused some IS departments to shrink in size is outsourcing. Outside companies are hired to perform one or more information tasks ranging from small applications to running an entire data center. Companies use outsourcing to reduce costs, obtain state-of-the-art technology, eliminate staffing problems, and to concentrate on the company's core business. The decision to outsource an entire systems operation is made by the CEO and information managers can do little about it. Outsourcing decisions for smaller projects might originate with the IS manager whose people are too involved in other projects to take new ones on. The downside of outsourcing is that companies may be asked to enter complicated, restrictive contracts that may make it difficult to change if the arrangement isn't working well. With major outsourcing comes downsizing. IS personnel are fired, and their knowledge, experience, and company loyalty is lost.

This chapter was designed to give some of the pros and cons of management and to describe the status and role of information managers today. It presented the management alternative to technical work and some of the requirements for those who choose this alternative. Still other alternatives will be presented in Chapter 8 for those who want to work for themselves rather than for someone else. The computer industry was built by just such entrepreneurs.

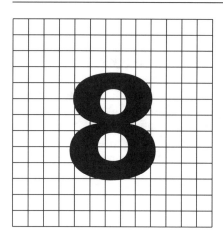

CAREERS IN CONSULTING, CONTRACTING, ENTREPRENEURSHIP, AND EDUCATION

Today's top business school graduates are aggressively pursued by large corporations regardless of the state of the economy. Companies realize that their futures depend on this influx of talent to keep them competitive in a dynamic business environment. But the attitudes of graduates from the top ranked business schools are changing. While 25 percent of Columbia University's MBAs went to work for large manufacturers in 1990, only 13 percent did in 1994. In 1989, 70 percent of Stanford's business graduates joined large companies compared to 50 percent in 1994. Where are these bright young people going? Estimates show that about half the students at top schools go to work for management consulting firms or investment bankers after graduation, with an intention to become entrepreneurs when they have gained the necessary money and experience. However, Microsoft and a number of other high-tech firms are still getting their share of the top graduates. The reason is that they offer growth, variety, and challenge.

The variety and challenge of jobs in computer fields reach a peak in this chapter. For the most part, the positions discussed require individuals with experience in one or more of the areas of work already described. Consulting, contracting, and entrepreneurship provide opportunities for individuals to work for themselves. According to a recent survey of senior business majors at a large eastern university, most students considered operating one's own business to be the best means to attain their goals. This chapter will investigate some interesting career alternatives for independent thinkers and experienced professionals.

OPPORTUNITIES IN CONSULTING

In 1993 alone over 80,000 consultants, ranging from those with huge global companies to individuals working from their basements, did $17 billion worth of business, according to a *Business Week* July 25, 1994, article. Information managers use consulting services widely to stay competitive in an environment of constantly changing technology. Such tasks as selecting equipment to meet both current and future needs, setting up massive computer and communications systems, and reengineering the company organization and work procedures to implement the new technology are often beyond the abilities of in-house staff. The risk is so great and the cost is so large that managers look to experts to help them make the right decisions. Contract programming, disaster recovery, and systems integration are among services provided by outsiders such as information or professional services firms, consultants, and contract programmers. This trend is likely to continue.

In good humor, consultants have been defined as professionals who have been out of work for more than two months. And regarding their work: consultants borrow your watch, then tell you what time it is. Humor aside, consultants provide a valuable service in a constantly changing field. Consultants in information fields may work for themselves as individual freelance specialists; for small firms with staffs of specialists; for large accounting firms, such as Arthur Anderson & Co., whose division Anderson Consulting is the leader in information systems consulting; for large, multidisciplinary research and consulting organizations, such as Arthur D. Little, Inc.; or for any type of organization or industry as an internal consultant.

The Work of Information and Communications Consultants

Consultants are usually specialists in management, communications, or information systems development with expertise in such highly specific fields as computer performance enhancement, computer security, project management, hardware and software selection, database management, telecommunications, and a number of other areas. A big area of demand for consultants today is systems integration, which provides for a client's total hardware and software needs. To work in this area, consultants must have had a wide range of experience. Such technical services as systems design, programming, documentation, technical training, and many others are often required by companies. Management services include market research, management information systems development, recruiting, productivity improvement, and too many others to list. Finally, hardware services such as equipment selection, installation evaluation, and facilities planning are also needed. In great demand today are former IS managers, top-notch systems analysts, technical writers who can write excellent documentation and training materials, telecommunications and database specialists, and computer security experts.

The primary work of the consultant is to structure and solve problems. Since consultants work for many clients, they gain exposure to different methods of solving problems and have a variety of valuable sources of information. Through this diverse experience, the consultant can eliminate alternatives that won't work and suggest those that have worked in similar circumstances, saving a client both time and money. A certain amount of freedom to do the job as seen fit, plus the image as expert, lend a good bit of status to the consultant's role. However, personal effectiveness is essential for doing further work for the client or being referred to other clients.

Working for a Consulting Firm

Top consulting firms hire graduates from the best business schools and then train them. These firms also offer summer internships to promising candidates and evaluate these recruits before offering them permanent employment with the firm. If a firm really wants a promising MBA candidate it will offer a well-paid summer internship after the first year, and pay the second year tuition if the student agrees to sign on after graduation. This could be as much as $30,000 depending on the school.

Work in large consulting firms is characterized by pressure, long hours, travel, and high turnover. These are partnerships that follow an *up-or-out policy*; that is, consultants have from five to seven years to make partner. If they fail, they are out. Only one in five who begin work with a large company are expected to make partner. Many opt for consulting with large firms for the training and experience, then go out on their own by choice. Most consulting firms are based in the Northeast and California. Larger firms have branches throughout the country.

Clients often retain consultants on a continuing basis—especially in information and communication systems areas—so consulting work tends to be long term. Entry-level consulting work in large companies is primarily research. As junior consultants or associates demonstrate the technical, analytic, and interpersonal skills required for success in the job, they are promoted to the position of case team leader or senior consultant. In this capacity a consultant supervises a small team normally working on one or two cases at a time. Three or four years later, if the senior consultant is performing well, he or she is promoted to consulting manager. As manager, a consultant leads a consulting team on important client projects. Once promoted to junior partner and finally senior partner or director, the consultant's work is primarily marketing the firm and its services. Figure 8.1 shows a career path in a large consulting firm.

Though beginners may be hired out of college with undergraduate degrees, an MBA is required by most firms for advancement. Most beginners earn $28,000 to $34,000 a year with mid- and end-of-year bonuses. College graduates with two years of experience can earn approximately $50,000 plus bonuses. MBAs earn salaries in the range of $45,000 to $90,000. Competition is heating up among large consulting firms in recruiting top graduates. Recently, a top MBA graduate was offered a $95,000 base salary, a $20,000 signing bonus, and a fully-loaded laptop computer. Beginning consultants with MBAs from top business schools such as Harvard and Stanford earn $60,000 plus bonuses. Salaries increase dramatically with promotions. Junior partners earn in excess of $150,000 plus bonuses and shares in the firm.

Figure 8.1   Career Path in a Large Consulting Firm

Senior partners earn from $300,000 to $600,000, with the most senior earning salaries in excess of $1 million.

Independent Consulting   The number of small consulting operations with no more than three people has doubled between 1991 and 1993. The consultant competes with other consultants for jobs. Companies usually invite several consultants in for interviews. Who is hired depends on two things. The first is how well the interviewer and consultant get along personally. The second is the quality of the consultant's references including companies for whom he or she has satisfactorily completed an assignment similar in nature to the one proposed.

A contract is then drawn up specifying the assignment, a plan for conducting and controlling the project, a description of what items the consultant agrees to deliver, starting and ending dates, and the fee. The fee is usually fixed, but in cases where this is impossible, a range of fees may be established. In addition, the contract includes payment procedures and a confidentiality clause to protect any company information given to the consultant in the course of the assignment.

The successful consultant is aggressive and willing to go out and hustle business. This alone is hard work. Consulting is not the job for someone who wants to work less and avoid the eight-to-five routine. Longer, though less-routine, hours are required for successful consulting. Also, although consultants are fairly well paid when they do work, there are times when they don't. Those who freelance or work as partners in small firms must have the financial resources to manage during tough times. This is another factor along with the required experience that suggests consulting is for the well-established professional. Self-employed consultants must earn 50 percent more than their large-firm counterparts to pay for the costs of doing business and the benefits normally provided by the company, such as health insurance, paid holidays and vacations, travel expenses, office space, supplies and equipment, clerical help, and telephone expenses.

As mentioned already, a consultant has to be willing to hustle for jobs. One way to do this is to become known from publishing articles in trade journals. Still another way is to become actively involved in professional organizations, thus meeting many potential clients. Efforts can't end here. Using former clients to identify potential clients, consultants must market their services to executives with the power to hire them. Consultants who want to run their consulting as a small business and maintain independent contractor status in the eyes of the Internal Revenue Service may use broker firms (which operate something like headhunters) to find consulting jobs. The broker earns from twenty-five to forty percent of what the consultant is paid on the initial contact with the hiring company, and less in subsequent contacts.

Like management, independent consulting is not for everyone. But if one has expertise in a sought-after area of specialization, can sell himself or herself, is financially well-off enough to survive the lean times, and wants the challenge and freedom of consulting, my advice is to go for it! Those who are unsuccessful can always give up the business and find a salaried job. It is easier to recover from a loss of self-esteem if a person is gainfully employed.

OPPORTUNITIES IN CONTRACTING

Contract programmers agree to provide software under a contractual arrangement for companies both inside and outside the computer industry. In a sense, they are a subset of consultants providing a specific service, namely programming. Some people make the following distinction between consultants and contractors. Consultants analyze a situation, propose a solution, but do not implement it. Contractors implement predefined solutions.

Many of the same things written about consultants is true for contractors. They must understand how to market their services and work hard at it. Having financial resources to cover themselves during the lean times and to pay for health insurance, office supplies, phone bills, and other expenses is important. A difference between consulting and contracting is that any creative individual with good programming skills can make some money programming; from teenagers to those with years of experience, from the physically handicapped to the most athletic, from the totally self-employed to the moonlighters. This is true because of the tremendous demand for software to keep pace with rapidly changing technology.

It is difficult to say how much software is written by program contractors today because much of their work is done off the books. Equally hard to determine is how many of these freelancers support themselves solely through contracting or are moonlighters. Industry experts believe that half of the nation's full-time programmers moonlight. Another estimate states that one-third of all programmers think seriously of going into business for themselves and about one half of them actually do it.

There is increasing demand for specific types of applications software. Applications software written both in the old and the new nonprocedural languages, network software, database software, software for the exploding personal computer market, and interactive entertainment are all in demand. Since writing software is costly and time-consuming, software firms are finding a good market for their packaged software. Customers are paying $100,000 for software that would cost several times that much to develop in-house. Software publishers buy or develop software, then package and market it. Rather than working for an hourly rate or a set price, as does the contractor working for a user company, those who write programs for sale by a software vendor usually receive royalties for their work, as do authors of books. The expanding software industry offers contract programmers many opportunities to develop software in their areas of interest and expertise.

Program contractors don't have to conform to rules and regulations. Unlike the consultant, image is not important. Many work at home and dress however they like. This is especially true in the personal computer market. Paul Lutus lived alone in the woods, wrote programs, and earned six-figure royalties. Most of these royalties came from a word processing program called "Apple Writer" that earned millions for Apple Computer, Inc. A high-school dropout with a very high IQ, Paul Lutus still does his own thing—and he does it very well. This, of course, is the key to writing and selling software as a freelancer: having the skill to satisfy a particular need and doing it very well.

ENTREPRENEURSHIP

The computer industry was built by single-minded, pioneering entrepreneurs with salable ideas for high-technology products. These pioneers and the venture capitalists who backed them were the risk takers who gambled that computerization was the wave of the future. Successes are legend: Microsoft, IBM, Apple, and so on. Entrepreneurs have been the driving force behind the rapid growth of the computer industry in the United States with its technological lead over other countries. Some successful entrepreneurs want a new challenge or find they do not enjoy or are not well suited to managing once-small companies that have grown large, so they sell their interests in the company and start another one.

Opportunities abounded in the past because of the rapidly changing technology and the willingness of venture capitalists to sink lots of money into new high-tech businesses. After a first success, an entrepreneur was able to bargain for a larger share of the second company. Many sources of venture capital have dried up and it isn't as easy for a beginner to find financing, but then those who built the industry were beginners. The information systems industries have always attracted many entrepreneurs—bright, creative, independent people with new ideas. Many individuals in information industries have lost their jobs through shutdowns, cutbacks, and mergers. Some of these have used their acquired experience and talent to start their own businesses or consult for others.

The Entrepreneur

Over two million new businesses were formed in 1993, 20 percent of which were one- or two-person operations. Some new business start-ups were by those who lost their jobs as a result of downsizing, but most were by individuals seeking a better quality of life than they are able to find working for someone else. This new generation of entrepreneurs is better educated and is starting more sophisticated businesses than in previous years. Many of their companies provide consulting or business services to other businesses, using affordable, powerful computers and telecommunications equipment.

It has been said that the only way most people are ever going to make a million dollars is by starting their own businesses. Realistically, most of today's small businesses provide only a modest living for their owners. The majority will go out of business within the first three years. Still the contribution of small business to the U.S. economy is dramatic. Small businesses account for about half of the nonfarm, nongovernmental employment in the country. Over the past six years they have generated about 44 million jobs. However, apart from job creation, entrepreneurial companies spur large ones to make innovations in products and to create new markets. And some, such as Microsoft, grow very large themselves.

Braving the risk of failure, entrepreneurs start businesses for the following reasons—to use skills or abilities, to gain control over their lives, to build for their families, for the challenge of it, to live the way they want or in the place they want, to gain respect or recognition, to earn lots of money, to fulfill other's expectations, or as the best alternative available. Women have been starting businesses at twice the rate of men. More African-Americans are starting their own companies with help from a black business network of powerful contacts.

Entrepreneurs Start With a Good Idea

Entrepreneurs find a market niche and develop a product. Sue Rugge not only started a business but a new field when she lost her job as a corporate librarian—information brokering. Information brokers are researchers who find information via computer for their customers. With over 3,000 commercial databases available, these professionals can locate whatever specific information is required. Manual and on-line searches, report writing, research and analysis, company profiles, information on competitors, and bibliographies are among the services they might provide. Fees range from $50 to $100 an hour. Research skills, familiarity with databases, and knowledge in a particular industry are needed for work in this field.

W. S. "Spider" Webb started Office Systems Consultants, which helps companies plan the best way to store their records. Alternatives can include color-coded file folders in shelving, movable shelving or rotary power files, a microfilm system, a digital imaging system with optical disk or CDs, or a combination of different systems. Technology has offered new solutions to an old problem and "Spider" Webb offers these to his clients.

Two local network services provide Tallahassee with efficient and cheaper access to Internet. SymNet and SuperNet offer the public specialized connections (SLIPs and PPPs) that provide a graphic interface when using Internet. Tallahassee FreeNet has so many subscribers per line that it has become impractical for business purposes because of the wait. The entrepreneurs saw the need and filled it.

Succeeding as an Entrepreneur

The entrepreneur has the freedom to run the company in his or her own way. However, small businesses are built on more than dreams of money and independence. A tremendous amount of knowledge and effort is involved. The entrepreneur needs total commitment to the business, freedom from family responsibilities, a tolerance for hard work, good health, and strong ethical standards. Starting a business is difficult; staying in business is harder still.

The prospective entrepreneur must secure financing for the proposed venture, usually from relatives, friends, and lending institutions. Normally entrepreneurs put a good bit of their own money into their businesses. Given the idea is good, raising capital for high-tech businesses is somewhat easier than for other small businesses. This is not to say that many high-tech businesses do not go under. But the growth and potential profits in high-tech areas are appealing enough to venture capitalists to offset the risk if an impressive business plan is presented. Venture capital firms are groups of investors who extend financial backing annually to 30,000 to 40,000 start-up companies in return for part ownership of the company. Usually the venture capital firm wants to protect its investment by having considerable say in how the company is run.

Once the financial backing is obtained, the entrepreneur begins planning, accounting, purchasing, producing, marketing, managing, and staffing the business. This requires a good general knowledge of the activities of business as well as the technical knowledge essential to the project. Such attributes as a willingness to face risk, to work long hours, to tolerate the uncertainty of success during the early stages of the business, and to keep very thorough records in order to fill in the innumerable forms required by the government, are all needed to be a successful entrepreneur.

A tremendous amount of sales ability also is needed, not only to raise the capital but to attract employees willing to risk job security in a newly formed company and to sell goods to customers being constantly bombarded with newer, supposedly better products. The entrepreneur is of a rare breed, both resilient and tough—flexible enough to change plans when advantageous and strong enough to handle the disappointments and problems that plague all who go into business for themselves.

Franchise Ownership

Many who want to own their own small businesses—but have neither an original idea nor the business acumen to start a business from scratch—choose to buy a franchise. A franchise can be defined as an agreement between a small business owner and a parent company that gives the owner the right to handle the company's product or service under conditions agreed upon by both. The store itself also is called a franchise. Franchises are in over 65 areas of business and generate close to $800 billion in sales every year. Growth has been declining somewhat as markets become crowded. In the past, statistics tended to show the proportionate number of failures among franchises to be significantly less than among other independent businesses. Other studies have found the failure rate to be about the same—high.

Certain advantages to franchises help minimize the risk of failure. Training and assistance from the parent company in setting up shop, choosing a location, estimating the potential sales, and designing marketing strategies are very helpful to the new owner. Another advantage to franchises is the benefit of having a nationally-known name and tested products. Cooperative buying power enables the franchisee to get supplies at lower costs, and sometimes credit assistance. These advantages do not guarantee success. In the volatile computer industry even parent companies sometimes fail, bringing down all franchise stores as well.

There are costs associated with a franchise which include some or all of the following: a franchising fee, a percentage of the profits of the business, and an agreement that products or equipment will be purchased from the vendors specified by the franchiser. In the relationship between franchiser and franchisee, the bargaining position of the franchisee is far less than that of the franchiser. Thus caution should be exercised before entering into an agreement.

Some general guidelines for computer professionals interested in franchises such as computer stores are as follows. Before entering into an agreement, a business owner should carefully read the prospectus provided by the parent company and get legal advice as well. Potential profits should be assessed by questioning other franchisees and objective sources. The Federal Trade Commission requires that franchisers divulge any litigation in which they are involved. Complaints filed with the Federal Trade Commission against parent companies have been growing more than 50 percent annually since 1990 and are now in the hundreds. All the details of such litigation should be known by the prospective franchisee. The franchisee should also obtain his or her own land and lease-hold improvement costs and not rely solely on the franchiser's estimates. Return on investment should be calculated using the prospective franchisee's figures. Remember that the franchiser is in business to sell franchises and is bound to make them look as attractive as possible. As more computer-related franchises become available and more computer professionals see them as a way to tap into the huge industry profits, there will be more cases of abuse, lack of business ethics, and disappointments for those who enter franchise agreements unaware of some of the pitfalls.

OPPORTUNITIES IN EDUCATION

Demand is excellent for educators to prepare computer professionals for all of the careers discussed in this book. These educators, depending on their backgrounds, are employed by colleges and universities, vocational and technical schools, high schools, specialized computer schools, and computer vendors. They usually are trained both in educational techniques and computers. Many of these educators, as well as other computer professionals, also write books, including textbooks for use in classes and trade books for the general public.

College and University Teaching

Professional educators may find teaching positions in community colleges. A master's degree is usually sufficient qualification for a position in a community college. Depending on supply and demand, a doctorate might be required and is always preferred. A doctorate in Management Information Systems or Computer Science is always required for tenure-track positions in four-year colleges and universities. Earning one's doctorate requires a large commitment of time and money. Applicants must not only hold a Master's degree, but must demonstrate the potential for conducting original research. Doctoral programs require at least two years of full-time coursework and seminars along with the design and completion of a doctoral dissertation. This can be a lengthy process depending on the project design, and each step must be approved by a committee before the candidate may go on. A review of the literature, design of the project, data gathering or laboratory experimentation, and an analysis of results can take well over a year to complete.

Instructors in two-year schools primarily teach but may be expected to write books and articles as well. University professors normally have lighter teaching loads but are required to publish articles in their field as a requirement for promotion and tenure. In addition, both instructors and professors are evaluated on service to their schools, which usually includes serving on committees and can involve fund-raising. Assistant professors are promoted to associate professor, then full professor. Often college professors enter administrative positions such as department chairman or dean. Such posts as dean of undergraduate or graduate business studies or dean of the college of business are filled by former professors. Figure 8.2 shows the hierarchy of a typical university college of business. Professors in computer

Figure 8.2   University College of Business Hierarchy

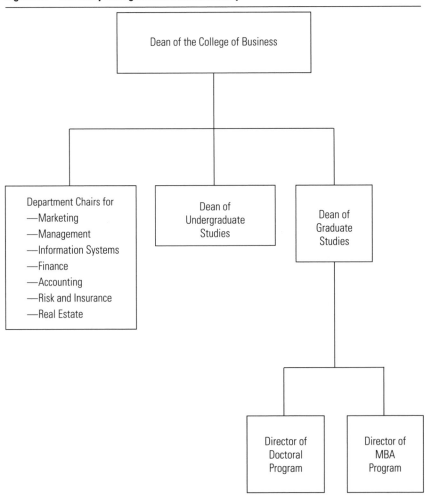

science departments which may be in the college of arts and sciences would be part of a similar hierarchy. It is not unusual for professors to earn money outside the university as consultants or entrepreneurs.

User Training

Another educational area is user training. The current emphasis on computer literacy in elementary and secondary schools assures opportunities for educators to work at that level and other educators to train them to do it. In fact, every elementary student is receiving some hands-on computer experience today. However, many adults have not yet been exposed to user education. It is not unheard of for the prompt, "Press any key to continue," to elicit the response, "Where's the ANY key?" Hundreds of training companies have found training to be a lucrative business, especially in the personal computer market. Computer educators can offer training and seminars as freelancers or be employed by computer stores, educational and training institutions, computer vendors, and user companies.

SOURCES OF INFORMATION

Numerous publications are available to those interested in consulting as a profession. Consultants are listed in a number of directories, including *Dun's Consultant's Directory* and *Consultants and Consulting Organizations Directory*, found in the reference section of the library. *Consultants News* and *Journal of Management Consulting* are periodicals covering up-to-date information in the field. Some associations for consultants are listed below:

American Consultants League
1290 Palm Avenue
Sarasota, FL 34236
(813) 952-9290

American Association of Professional Consultants
9140 Ward Parkway
Kansas City, MO 64114
(913) 681-3242

Council of Consulting Organizations
521 5th Avenue, Thirty-fifth floor
New York, NY 10175-3598
(212) 697-9693

The growth of franchising can be seen in *Entrepreneur* magazine's annual *Franchise 500* issue which lists 873 franchisers. The *Franchise Opportunities Handbook*, published by the Bureau of Industrial Economics and Minority Business Development Agency of the United States Department of Commerce, can be found in the government documents section of most libraries. Published monthly, it includes not only a list of available franchises but excellent tips for prospective franchise owners, such as a checklist for evaluating a franchise, financial assistance information, and a sizable list of sources of franchising information. The Small Business Administration, with offices in all major cities, is another excellent source of information for those interested both in franchises and in independent ventures. Other sources include the following:

International Franchise Association
1350 New York Avenue, NW
Suite 900
Washington, DC 20005
202-628-8000

Directory of Franchise Business Opportunities
Franchise Business Opportunities Publishing Company
1725 Washington Road
Suite 205
Pittsburgh, PA 15241

Directory of Franchising Organizations
Pilot Industries, Incorporated
347 Fifth Avenue
New York, NY 10016

The Franchise Annual
Info Press
736 Center Street
Lewiston, NY 14092

The directories listed above are revised annually and provide information on many franchise opportunities. These franchises should be thoroughly checked out by contacting both the Better Business Bureau and the International Franchise Association. Many excellent books on franchising are on the market, a number of them available through the International Franchise Association itself.

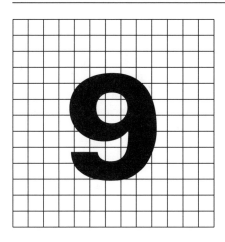

OPPORTUNITIES FOR WOMEN, MINORITIES, TEENS, PEOPLE WITH DISABILITIES, AND THE ELDERLY

Technology has opened the door to opportunities in all fields for those of all ages. Telecommuting offers special opportunities to women, people with disabilities, and any others who need to work from the home or a neighborhood center. The term encompasses everything from occasional work at home to permanent work arrangements away from the office. The concept of telecommuting is catching on for a number of reasons. Pressure exists in some municipalities to reduce the number of employees commuting by car to work each day; many workers are unable to balance family and work obligations; management, unable to offer workers the traditional promotions and raises, must find new ways to reward them. Telecommuting gives companies the flexibility to accommodate and retain their most productive workers. In fact, according to research conducted by Miller Associates, a market research firm in Ithaca, New York, workers telecommuting from home or neighborhood work centers are 10 to 20 percent more productive than when they work from the office. Lack of distractions and interruptions is a major advantage of telecommuting.

Many careers in the information field lend themselves to independent work outside the office and everyone has a chance at them without being subjected to as many traditional sex, race, age, and other types of biases. This is not to say that placement in computer careers is free from any of this type of discrimination. But because of a number of factors, this discrimination is less than most other career areas.

One factor that has contributed to a positive record for employing women and minorities is that the personal computer industry is less than 20 years old, with the average age of employees under 40. Its growth has occurred concurrently with many consciousness-raising activities in the area of equal employment opportunity, such as the development of the women's movement and the

Equal Employment Opportunity Commission. Another factor is the demand for skilled personnel in rapidly growing computer fields. Managers have not been in a position to overlook the talent of women and minorities. They have had to focus on getting enough qualified people to do the job. This will be even more a factor because the workforce is becoming more diverse. According to the Bureau of Labor Statistics, percentage makeup in the workforce is changing. It is projected that between 1990 and 2005 the percentage of white workers will decline while percentages of blacks, Asians, and Hispanics will increase. Between those years the percentage of male workers will decline as female workers increase.

Opportunities to work in information careers exist both in companies and at home. Networking and personal computers make it possible for those who can work only at home to hold a job and receive a competitive salary for doing it. In addition, temporary services offer an alternative to full-time permanent positions. Temporary service firms have expanded from offering low-skill workers for emergency fill-in positions to workers with computer skills who may be hired routinely to meet business fluctuations or to complete an entire project headed by a temporary manager. Automation skills make up a large portion of the business of temporary service firms.

OPPORTUNITIES FOR WOMEN

Women and computers go back a long way. In fact, the first programmer was a nineteenth-century noblewoman, Lady Augusta Ada Byron Lovelace. Having tremendous mathematical abilities, she wrote papers describing Charles Babbage's *analytical engine,* the forerunner of the modern computer. She described the concepts of "loops" and "subroutines" a century before their implementation in electronic digital computers. Another woman widely known for her work with computers is Captain Grace Hopper of the United States Navy. Captain Hopper has worked with computers from their vacuum tube days to the present, and she is considered an expert in the area.

In general, women have been very successful in computer fields. Entry into these fields is easier than many others because of the demand. Data-entry jobs require a minimum of formal education, but are not always dead-end jobs. Opportunities arise for data-entry operators to learn programming and thus advance somewhat in the company. Most people agree that establishing effective modes of communication within the company is the key to advancement. Thus women help one another to gain inside information and make crucial business contacts. Women have organized their own professional organizations, some of which are listed in Chapter 11.

Women are somewhat underrepresented in management positions within the computer industry itself. Even so, most women feel that computer fields are wide open and opportunities abound. One study showed that more and more women are opting for computer programming and technical management jobs. Women show a willingness to take entry-level jobs, and this push from the bottom is helping women finally make it into management positions.

Successful women state that in order to get ahead, women must have good business sense and a broad background in business so they can understand how the company makes money. This is true, of course, for men as well. Success stories over the past decade include that of Lois Martin, who in nine years advanced from systems analyst to vice-president of operations at the First National Bank of St. Paul, Minnesota. Another successful woman, Patricia G. Karolchyk, worked for Texaco for thirteen years in technical project management before accepting the position as director of technical planning at American Express. Within four years, she advanced into line management as vice-president of systems planning and development for American Express's Consumer and Financial Services Group in Europe. Within the computer industry, Carol Bartz is CEO of Autodesk of Sausalito, California. Sandra Kurtzig founded the software company ASK Group. In government, Mary Lowe Good holds the position of undersecretary for technology at the Commerce Department, and Arati Prabhakar heads the National Institute of Standards and Technology.

Every new woman who enters top management opens doors for other talented women. Women seeking employment should learn which positions in management are held by women in the companies where they are being interviewed. A skepticism of women's managerial abilities by top management might be reflected in an absence of women managers.

Despite the facts that computer careers offer many opportunities for women and that the computer industry has been more aggressive and successful in hiring talented women that most others, there are a couple of factors that may work against women. Among these are the limited expectations many women have regarding their futures. Some advice for women includes establishing a specific career plan, keeping up with what is happening in computer fields as a whole, taking advantage of career development or special management training programs for women, considering all career opportunities both inside and outside data processing, staying aware of other talented women coming up through the ranks, and using career strategies for advancement.

Another factor that may impact negatively on women's progress in computer fields is that, as children, boys exhibit greater enthusiasm for computers than girls. To verify this, notice that the number of boys in video arcades, computer camps, and after-school sessions on computers greatly exceeds that of the girls. Since girls do as well as boys on computer literacy tests, the amount of enthusiasm seems cultural in nature. Reasons for this include biased parents, the linguistic orientation of girls and the math orientation of boys, male-oriented computer advertising, and so on. It is important that girls as well as boys begin to acquire computer skills early if they are to hold leadership positions as adults.

OPPORTUNITIES FOR MINORITIES

As is the case with women, the computer marketplace has done a better job of hiring minority candidates than other fields. Asian Americans have been highly successful. The number of key positions they hold is very high in proportion to their representation in the industry. Hispanics have also done very well. Although blacks have been somewhat underrepresented in the past, this is lessening as those who have entered computer fields gain experience and help recruit other blacks. Emphasis on the development of math skills with black youths is needed.

Computer Mart, Inc., a chain of franchised computer stores, was founded in 1976 by Rick Inatome, the son of Japanese–American parents. Inatome turned the $35,000 he borrowed on his father's life insurance into a yearly six-figure salary, and his family shared his success. His father helped set up an international branch of Computer Mart to sell computers in the Middle East, his mother served as secretary of the corporation, and his brother was responsible for opening new stores.

Many of the qualities that minorities need for success are rarely taught in schools. Such business sense as how to set priorities is important. Determining what is important to the organization—that is, how it makes its money—is essential. Good communication and leadership skills also are important. These qualities, in combination with five years of technical experience, have earmarked many minority members for management positions in larger organizations or as managers of their own companies.

OPPORTUNITIES FOR PEOPLE WITH DISABILITIES

Because computer programming is an activity that engages the mind rather than the body, it has been a very promising career for the physically challenged. Adaptive technology includes hardware and software products that even individuals who cannot use a mouse or a keyboard can operate. This includes rearranging workstations, making keyboard modifications, or using alternative input devices. Computer technology has enabled the handicapped and homebound to work in a number of areas such as accounting, bookkeeping, and fields that permit outside contact via telephone, telefacsimile, and computer terminal. Microprocessors and minicomputers are being used to control the operation of typewriters, tape recorders, telephones, television, lighting, appliances, wheelchairs, limb prostheses, and manipulators. The research and training center of the National Institute of Handicapped Research has developed an entire office environment that can be run by a quadriplegic using a computer-controlled system.

Speech recognition devices provide telephone access to deaf users, and Braille typewriters and line printers allow computer use by blind programmers. An alternative to the Braille line printer is Optacon, an optical-to-tactile converter. The user scans printed text on a display screen with a handheld camera while the tactile image of each symbol is presented to the finger of the other hand. Optacon has been used for years by blind computer-related professionals. VersaBraille II Plus, a more recent development, allows the user to move the standard cursor along the screen as Braille letters pop up in a small windowed surface on the desktop VersaBraille machine.

A more efficient method of receiving output for the blind user is via voice generators. These synthetic speech devices allow the computer to "talk" to the programmer. The voice generator can "read" the screen and convert displayed text into speech output, both pronouncing and spelling out words. The user can slow the pronunciation of misunderstood words. As more of these devices become available and the price goes down, job opportunities for blind programmers will expand. In addition to these output devices, voice programming has also been developed. The user talks to the voice programming system telling it what input data are selected and the system writes programs according to what it is told. As a result of a gun accident, Rick Pilgrim can move only his eyes and mouth. But each day he performs his programming job by speaking COBOL to his personal computer.

Ronald Pulleybank can neither move nor speak, yet he creates programs for Hewlett–Packard laboratories. This is possible through use of a Words Plus Software Keyboard Emulator. Using a camera attached to his head and the emulator, he is able to select a letter through maintaining his gaze for a second. Headmaster is a head-mounted optical pointer that enables the user to move the cursor to a desired position by moving the head and then blowing through a tube to activate a puff switch mounted on the headset. Scanning is a method by which the computer advances the cursor row by row until the user activates a switch, then letter by letter until the desired key is reached and the switch is again activated as a key press.

IntroVoiceV is a voice input system that enables the speaking handicapped to utter a command or series of commands or to verbally cause a string of text to appear on the screen. One gadget, a fully voice-controlled robot, enables a handicapped person to say "Get drink" and have the mechanical servant bring water.

There has been continuous progress in the development of devices to aid people with disabilities. Personal computers not only allow the handicapped to work but enable them to remain in close contact with people and activities through electronic mail. To foster this development, Johns Hopkins University, with grant support from the National Science Foundation and Radio Shack, conducted a contest. They held a nationwide search for ideas and inventions to aid the physically or mentally handicapped, including prototype devices, computer programs, and system designs. There were categories for computer professionals, amateurs, and students. A $10,000 grand prize was offered plus one hundred other prizes, which included several computing systems. The federal government recently passed legislation mandating that all computer equipment purchased by the federal government must be adaptable for use by the disabled. In addition, Congress passed a bill authorizing more than $15 million to develop and obtain assistive technologies for the disabled.

Many training programs have been developed for the handicapped in computer programming. The Association of Rehabilitation Programs in Data Processing (ARPDP) chooses students with cerebral palsy, arthritis, stroke impairments, paraplegia, and quadriplegia. Required for selection are a high-school diploma, above-average intelligence, and twelfth-grade-level reading and math skills.

Still another program sponsored by ARPDP is Lift, Inc. This nonprofit contract programming firm identifies, trains, and arranges programming contracts for its students with major corporations. These handicapped programmers work from home. Sometimes they are offered permanent jobs by the organizations that contracted for their services. The fee paid to Lift is competitive with other contract programming shops and the programmers receive a competitive wage as well. Lift accepts students that are more severely handicapped than those in other ARPDP programs. Superior programming courses are offered at the National Technical Institute for the Deaf in Rochester, New York; Disabled Programmers, Inc., in Campbell, California; and the Center for Independent Living in Berkeley, California. This training is designed to be better than what a regular student at an average technical school would get in order to improve a handicapped person's competitive position in the job market.

In general, the handicapped workers are extremely loyal and hardworking. Having the ability to overcome a handicap and gain training for a career requires tremendous dedication. This dedication transfers to the workplace when the handicapped worker is employed. In addition to gaining a dedicated, qualified worker, employers of the handicapped receive benefits from the government. The Revenue Act of 1978 allows employers to deduct fifty percent of the first $6,000 paid in wages during the first full year on the job and twenty-five percent in the second year. Also, the government allows the company up to $25,000 in write-offs for the removal of architectural barriers to the handicapped. Apart from the positive incentives to hire the handicapped, the 1973 Rehabilitation Act requires employers doing over $2,500 worth of business to take affirmative action in hiring handicapped workers and, according to law, no job applicant can be turned down solely because of his or her handicap.

Tax credits also are offered to employers hiring the socially handicapped. Ex-felons who received data processing skills in such prisons as San Quentin, Leavenworth, and Terre Haute are now contributing to society. An early study of these programs showed that twenty inmates at San Quentin, who accumulated over two-thousand hours of programming experience between 1974 and 1980, have all done very well on the outside. Not one returned to crime in over two years since their release.

OPPORTUNITIES FOR TEENS AND THE ELDERLY

The generation that is growing up with computers is also growing wealthier with them. Young entrepreneurs, ages twelve to twenty, are turning their command of computer programming into sizable profits by writing software. Their imagination and enthusiasm have given them the edge over work-weary, time-constrained adults in the development of games. In past years, talented teens have earned royalties in six-digit figures for developing popular games. The demand for these games has increased every year, making electronic games one of the fast growing segments in the computer industry.

The accomplishments of the microteens have not been in the development of games alone. Eugene Volokh at fourteen designed a computerized film-distribution system for Twentieth Century Fox. Steve Grimm and Nikolai Weaver at twelve years of age created Filewriter, a record-keeping system. Phil Oliver adapted a simplified computer language called PILOT for home computer use. With his royalties, Phil started his own company. Michael Dell took IBM PCs apart and rebuilt them with upgrade parts as a freshman in college. Before long he began selling both upgrade parts and rebuilt computers. Recognizing a market, in 1984 he began Dell Computer Corp. before the age of 20 with $1,000, selling computers directly to end users. Today, eleven years later, Dell could potentially get half of the direct computer sales which is projected to grow $8 to $10 billion annually. Dell's company is one of the country's top personal computer companies. The success stories go on and on. These successes can be at least partially attributed to the originality of youth and the absence of the pessimism of old age. All things are possible in the world of computers.

Microsoft's Bill Gates started young and has built the number one company in the industry. Never underestimating the imagination of the young, Gates sponsors a contest for nine- to eleven-year-olds in which they are asked to submit essays describing what the "coolest" computers could do. The six winners out of 10,000 entrants win a trip to Seattle to tour Microsoft and to meet Bill Gates, and a computer with a CD–ROM drive. Some of their ideas include programs that would recreate extinct animals that would answer questions about how they became extinct; record memories from a person's brain so bad memories and nightmares could be erased; scan people's optic nerves so they could see out of one another's eyes; baby-sit and even reproduce a hologram of Mom so baby wouldn't cry; help young people make job choices; and the suggestion from a deaf entrant—a portable computer that could change speech into words.

The elderly are not to be excluded from computer career opportunities either. Eric Knudson began his software company, ACS America, Inc., to capitalize on the work ethic of retired senior citizens and their talents. Knudson developed training centers and recruited those fifty-five years or older. If able to pass a programming aptitude test, the applicant was given three months free training and hired by ACS America as a subcontractor. These subcontractors are not given such fringe benefits as health or life insurance, but most have this from Medicare and health plans from previous employers. What the retirees gain is a new skill, a way to make extra money, and a productive way to spend their time. Opportunities abound for older workers in temporary service firms. Kelly Services has begun the ENCORE program to attract older workers and retirees to temporary service jobs. Information kits are distributed to organizations for retirees and seniors outlining the advantages of temporary work.

WORKING AT HOME

Apart from the millions of Americans who work full-time for companies and bring work home from time to time, there are three major categories of those who work at home: entrepreneurs who run small businesses from their homes, home-based employees who are electronically linked to the company office (telecommuters), and independent contractors. Of the estimated twenty-five million home office workers, about half are women and about six million are self-employed women. Women comprise about seventy percent of all home-based sole proprietorships. The breakdown of all people working from home is as follows: fifty percent are in professional or managerial occupations; thirty-three percent are in sales, technical, or administrative fields; and the other seventeen percent are in precision production, repair, and other assorted fields. Information-related service jobs will dominate home-office work.

The personal computer with its user-friendly operation, affordable prices, and variety of software has been the driving force behind this trend. Networks have made vast databases of information available through modems. Several economic factors have also contributed substantially to the growth in home-based work. Individuals laid off or retired early often start home-based businesses. Women with childcare responsibilities find working at home an alternative to expensive daycare centers and a way to spend more time with their children. Corporations can save money on office space and workplace maintenance using telecommuters and independent contractors. Convenience, flexibility, and economy will fuel the trend toward more home-based work.

Sources of information for home-based workers are:

American Home Business Association
397 Post Road
Darien, CT 06820
(800) 433–6361

Mothers' Home Business Network
P.O. Box 423
East Meadow, NY 11554
(516) 997–7394

National Association for the Cottage Industry
P.O. Box 14850
Chicago, IL 60614
(312) 472–8116

National Association of Home-Based Businesses
P.O. Box 30220
Baltimore, MD 21270
(410) 363–3698

National Association for the Self-Employed
P.O. Box 612067
Dallas, TX 75261–2067
(800) 551–4446

The following publications are available for purchase:

The Business Plan for Home-Based Businesses
SBA Publications
P.O. Box 30
Denver, CO 80201–0030

Home Office Computing, a monthly magazine
Scholastic, Inc.
555 Broadway
New York, NY 10012–3999

Numerous books on home-based businesses are available in your local library.

The message of this entire chapter is that anyone who has the ability to do the job can find meaningful work in computer careers both inside and outside the home. As long as demand remains high, this is likely to continue. This demand will be analyzed in the next chapter on the job market.

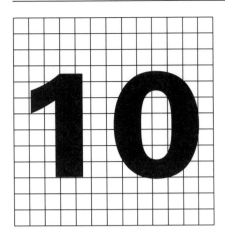

THE JOB MARKET
AND SALARY OUTLOOK

The U.S. economy on the whole is expected to continue growing at a moderate rate. Between now and the year 2005, there will be an average of 320,000 openings for college graduates. This figure is much larger than the past decade because of the openings created by the aging of the college-educated workforce. Computer engineers and scientists and systems analysts are among the top five fastest growing professions. Among the top forty growth jobs of the next decade are computer engineer, computer systems analyst, computer-operations researcher, and data-processing equipment repairer. Computer firms will offer many job opportunities as growth in the industry continues. Computer and data processing services will create 795,000 new jobs from 1992–2005, a 61 percent growth rate.

Organizations have been restructuring and shrinking the number of employees. Computer companies are among the leaders in this trend. Organizations have become much flatter as middle management positions have been gradually eliminated. The reduction of personnel now seems to be ending and information professionals are once more in demand. Greatest demand is for top-level executive talent and bright young entry-level employees with knowledge in the new technologies. Database, telecommunications, and networking technologies, along with the widespread use of personal computers, has had a large impact on all computer careers. Those with experience in these areas as well as client–server systems, multimedia systems, expert systems, imaging technology, OOPs, and CASE applications are in great demand.

JOB MARKET FACTORS

The rate of job creation in the economy as a whole has been low given the rate of economic growth. Some explanations for this are that the productivity gains through advanced technology experienced by many companies reduced the need for more employees, that uncertain economic conditions are causing employers to be cautious about adding new positions, and that hiring and firing costs may be growing. A couple of factors that have influenced the increased demand for information professionals are the dramatic increases in the number of personal computer systems in use today and advances in communications technology. The emphasis in the industry is research and development since new product development is the key growth factor.

Demand

The computer industry experienced steady layoffs from 1988 through 1993 because of economic conditions, restructuring of organizations, and more efficient use of technology. However, future growth in the industry is expected. The hiring hot spots will be in software companies, computer-services companies specializing in outsourcing, and information-services companies specializing in databases and networks. Bureau of Labor Statistics figures indicate computer careers are among the fastest growing. Table 10.1 indicates growth and decline in employment for occupations in the computer field. The figures in the table appeared in the *Occupational Outlook Quarterly* 1994 Spring issue.

Trends pinpointing the demand for specific areas of expertise mentioned in previous chapters can be summarized as follows: the increasing popularity of the personal computer has dramatically increased demand for those who can design, build, and develop software for it. Both individual consumers and companies will buy personal computers in increasing numbers. Specialists in communications, networks, and database technologies will be sought by every industry. Systems analysts and applications programmers with expertise in these areas as well as expert systems, systems integration, and image processing will be very much in demand. Multimedia programmers will find many opportunities. Network professionals including network managers, network systems integrators, and network consultants will be very much in demand by banks, insurance, financial-service companies, and others. Client–server designers and computer security experts will also be in demand.

Industries outside of the computer industry offering the most opportunities include financial services, consumer products, manufacturing, utilities, education, insurance, biotechnology, health care, and pharmaceuticals. Opportunities with the government will be in areas such as managing new storage technologies, databases, and networks.

Supply

Demand is one half of the job market picture; supply is the other half. Opportunities will continue to be abundant for computer professionals because supply will not keep pace with demand in most areas, particularly entry-level workers. As demand grows, a decline in the young adult population between the ages of sixteen and twenty-four will continue. With competition

Table 10.1   Growth in Occupations from 1992 to 2005

Engineering, science, and data processing managers	*32%*	*106,000*

The rapid growth in demand for data processing managers is due to the expansion in the computer and data services industry and the increased employment of systems analysts.

Management analysts and consultants	*43%*	*89,000*

This growth is primarily due to the incorporation of new technologies in organizations.

Electrical and electronics engineers	*24%*	*90,000*

The fastest growth in this occupation will be in computer and communications equipment design.

Computer scientists and systems analysts	*111%*	*737,000*

Those who hold degrees in computer science, computer engineering, information science, and information systems will be the primary beneficiaries of these many new positions.

Computer programmers	*30%*	*169,000*

The greatest number of positions will be in data processing services firms, software houses, and computer consulting businesses.

Adult education teachers	*32%*	*172,000*

Most openings will be in computer technology.

College and university faculty	*26%*	*214,000*

The best prospects will be in business, engineering, and computer science.

Engineering technicians	*19%*	*132,000*

This lower growth rate is due to defense cutbacks.

Computer and office machine repairers	*30%*	*43,000*

Growth in the demand for computer repairers will be much faster than average.

Information clerks	*32%*	*429,000*

Both full-time and part-time opportunities will be excellent due to general business expansion.

Manufacturing and wholesale sales representatives	*5%*	*78,000*

This slower than average growth is because of increased sales-force productivity made possible by the new technologies.

Decline in Occupations from 1992 to 2005

Computer and peripheral equipment operators	*−41%*	*−122,000*

The decentralization of computer operations and the resulting increase in the use of personal computers, networks, client–server systems, and integration software has reduced the need for these operators.

Typists, word processors, and data entry keyers	*−4%*	*−46,000*

Technology has rendered many positions unnecessary and the best opportunities will be for those with broad knowledge of office technology.

from business, universities, and the military, there will not be enough entry-level workers to go around.

A smaller entry-level labor force means a reduced supply of information personnel already in demand. Entry-level systems analysts and applications programmers educated in the new technologies will be able to pick and choose. To compensate for the supply and demand gap, companies are attempting to build systems and organizations requiring fewer people, increasing training efforts, and developing more attractive compensation packages to lure the young talent.

This bright picture for young, entry-level personnel has a more somber side for older workers. Promotions will continue to be more competitive because of larger numbers of middle-aged workers with obsolete skills, the need to staff lower-level jobs, and the current trend to reduce middle-management positions. Most older workers have neither the skills nor the inclination to postpone retirement to build system architectures.

The increasing number of women entering the labor force will easily be recruited not because of legislation but because of increasing demand and limited supply. This is also true for minorities and the handicapped. The new technologies will increase opportunities for the handicapped to participate in the workforce.

Attitudes of workers also are changing. More emphasis is being placed on lifestyle and quality of life. Workers are pressing for more flexible work schedules. Working at home, already practical because of computer technology, is likely to become even more common. Semiconductor and disk drive manufacturers are going to have a harder time persuading workers to commute from another county to their jobs in the Silicon Valley in California where the majority of these manufacturers are located. Some manufacturers have already relocated.

An important factor affecting supply is the small number of educators to staff programs of study in computer fields. Salaries are so much lower in education and training than in practice that educators are leaving education. Despite the shortage of qualified educators, the number of computer degree programs is rapidly increasing. Practitioners teaching part-time and mathematics instructors, however reluctant, are no doubt staffing many of the courses. But the shortage of educators is likely to continue to limit the supply of computer professionals.

SALARY

There are a number of factors along with supply and demand that affect salaries of computer professionals. Women tend to earn less than men even when job level, age, education, and work experience are the same. In addition, the failure of women to advance to higher levels given the number employed in information fields is apparent. However, with increasing demand there is indication that women are moving into some higher-paying jobs. In 1993, a poll showed women holding 42.9 percent of local area network manager positions compared with 31 percent in 1992.

Turnover does not alter the overall supply and demand picture, but it does have an impact on both mobility and salary. It is often by changing jobs that computer professionals advance in position and gain salary increases. This practice continues as long as demand is high. The more in demand the particular area of specialization, the more mobility an individual has and the higher salary he or she earns. An expert in high demand areas can negotiate a base salary from three to fifteen percent higher than his or her current salary.

Salaries vary with company size, industry, and geography. In addition, they may be affected by installation size and level of technological sophistication. The salary picture is complicated by all of these factors. As an installation becomes more sophisticated with more on-line systems, greater use of telecommunications technology, and more complex operating systems, salaries tend to rise. Although there is a tendency for size and sophistication to go hand in hand, this is not always the case. A small state-of-the-art shop may offer salaries closer to the high salary range typically offered by large installations.

According to *Datamation's* 1994 salary survey, the salary picture for computer careers is improving. Pay raises averaged only 3.9 percent in 1993 but averaged 4.3 percent in 1994. Table 10.2 shows information salaries by company size.

It has become harder and harder to generalize about salaries. Usually the larger the information systems budget, the higher the salaries of the computer professionals. Also, the higher the company revenues, the higher the salaries. Two other factors affect the salary picture: industry and geography. But these vary somewhat with each position.

Salaries of Recent College Graduates

The College Placement Council (CPC) keeps track of salary offers to recent college graduates. The January 1995 CPC Salary Survey shows the average yearly offers for those holding bachelor degrees in computer fields. Some salaries, by curriculum for graduates, were as follows:

Management Information Systems (MIS)	$30,692
Computer engineering	34,809
Electrical/electronics engineering	35,839
Computer science	32,303
Computer programming	28,033
Information sciences	31,448
Systems analysis	33,218

Masters degree holders earned salaries as follows:

Management Information Systems	$45,750
Computer engineering	41,250
Electrical/electronic engineering	42,278
Computer science	39,786

Industry and Geography

The industry offering the highest salaries to computer professionals is the computer industry. Salary only partially explains the lure of the computer industry. Computer vendors are able to attract qualified people because of excellent salary and benefit packages, training programs, and continued industry growth forecasts. Many information systems managers feel that computer vendors offer greater job security. Loss of jobs through company adoption of new technologies or mergers which are occurring across all industries have become a large threat to many information systems managers. Table 10.3 from the *Datamation* salary survey shows compensation for information jobs for different industry groups.

Table 10.2 1994 U.S. Information Technology (IT) Salaries by Company Size

	Under $50M	$51M-$500M	$501M-$1B	Over $1B
CIO/VP	$93,983	$104,497	$130,412	$130,606
Director	$65,657	$76,927	$81,169	$89,501
Manager/Supervisor	$52,898	$56,783	$56,740	$64,850
Application Development Manager	$57,222	$60,889	$60,924	$64,494
Application Designer	$48,452	$51,717	$49,533	$53,254
Application Developer	$45,955	$46,133	$45,994	$49,710
Project Manager	$52,641	$54,943	$56,237	$58,385
Project Leader	$50,702	$50,850	$51,889	$56,197
Senior Systems Analyst	$48,051	$48,523	$50,876	$51,181
Systems Analyst	$38,432	$42,633	$42,826	$43,405
Senior Programmer Analyst	$42,438	$44,207	$42,685	$44,852
Programmer	$33,766	$35,148	$34,694	$38,251
Computer Operator	$26,102	$25,073	$28,069	$28,277
Data Entry Clerk	$19,472	$21,150	$21,533	$22,532
Administrator	$49,039	$50,532	$56,265	$54,390
Database Analyst	$43,593	$45,417	$47,447	$47,398
Network Manager (LAN/WAN)	$45,073	$50,054	$53,937	$53,994
LAN Manager	$38,768	$45,890	$46,969	$48,360
Network Engineer	$38,379	$40,670	$44,020	$46,037
Help Desk Manager	$36,636	$41,494	$43,303	$49,574
Technical Support Analyst	$34,500	$36,108	$36,654	$39,461
Computer Hardware Engineer	$39,874	$38,305	$38,274	$43,571
PC Technician	$29,026	$30,806	$31,850	$35,464

Geography affects salaries since there are cost of living differences for different parts of the country. Table 10.4 from the *Datamation* survey reports salaries for selected geographical areas. Robert Half International, Inc. is one of the major recruiting firms for information professionals. The company has a wealth of information on demand for information professionals and salaries. For information, write:

> Robert Half International, Inc.
> P.O. Box 33597
> Kansas City, MO 64120

OTHER FACTORS IN JOB SELECTION

Salary is only part of the compensation picture. In response to employee demands, employers are offering better and more varied benefit packages that differ in value. Some of the following items plus numerous others might be included in the package: health insurance, dental insurance, life insurance, disability, vacation, sick leave, paid holidays, bonuses, pension

Table 10.3 1994 U.S. Information Technology (IT) Salaries by Industry

	Manufacturing	Banking/ Financial Services	IS Services	Retail	Government	Medical/ Legal Services	Transportation/ Utilities	Education	Construction/ Mining/ Agriculture	Other Services
CIO/VP	$115,829	$121,841	$139,336	$99,576	$93,136	$102,089	$161,352	$80,771	—	$117,731
Director	$78,473	$92,538	$88,839	$78,557	$71,456	$63,226	$77,792	$61,812	$85,000	$79,634
Manager/Supervisor	$57,299	$60,590	$66,454	$56,999	$57,636	$47,527	$57,623	$49,403	$54,375	$61,535
Application Development Manager	$62,913	$64,523	$64,564	$59,350	$58,128	$57,252	$61,315	$51,893	$60,000	$63,684
Application Designer	$54,765	$55,996	$50,486	$42,741	$51,410	$40,870	$51,481	$41,383	$48,000	$53,622
Application Developer	$47,186	$53,495	$46,139	$40,848	$46,422	$40,416	$48,018	$42,023	$35,000	$49,173
Project Manager	$52,735	$59,276	$60,369	$56,962	$53,379	$48,711	$58,346	$46,822	$65,000	$58,062
Project Leader	$50,323	$60,502	$53,658	$50,890	$50,089	$44,368	$50,878	$47,697	—	$55,157
Senior Systems Analyst	$49,561	$52,770	$51,411	$46,788	$48,173	$42,498	$50,880	$40,789	$62,586	$52,969
Systems Analyst	$42,361	$45,683	$42,638	$43,021	$40,656	$37,968	$43,378	$36,014	$45,000	$45,411
Senior Programmer Analyst	$43,599	$45,541	$43,604	$42,216	$46,769	$42,497	$42,624	$36,619	$37,381	$44,756
Programmer	$36,431	$38,913	$34,865	$32,744	$36,108	$30,457	$33,806	$30,926	$30,000	$37,715
Computer Operator	$26,411	$28,825	$23,323	$24,397	$27,347	$22,579	$26,679	$26,205	$20,286	$27,060
Data Entry Clerk	$19,976	$22,005	$19,022	$18,367	$22,434	$18,167	$24,762	$17,739	—	$21,402
Administrator	$53,308	$60,773	$52,710	$55,954	$49,798	$42,539	$54,374	$53,010	$58,000	$47,897
Database Analyst	$47,390	$51,166	$50,184	$41,955	$46,616	$37,603	$44,953	$41,865	$48,000	$43,573
Network Manager (LAN/WAN)	$52,066	$57,921	$50,987	$44,531	$50,621	$48,722	$50,601	$40,133	$50,000	$50,011
LAN Manager	$45,227	$51,363	$50,615	$38,329	$48,042	$38,279	$46,198	$34,547	$43,952	$45,620
Network Engineer	$41,905	$42,597	$43,606	$35,033	$42,957	$36,552	$42,008	$46,191	$40,000	$44,015
Help Desk Manager	$43,100	$43,743	$48,127	$39,073	$43,267	$38,195	$43,664	$35,432	$50,000	$43,213
Technical Support Analyst	$36,464	$38,714	$40,391	$35,764	$38,039	$29,528	$37,450	$30,506	$47,025	$35,469
Computer Hardware Engineer	$39,255	$42,442	$40,683	$39,787	$40,904	$31,603	$37,146	$37,838	$40,000	$42,945
PC Technician	$31,643	$35,217	$31,905	$35,813	$32,044	$27,511	$29,332	$27,304	$40,000	$33,715

Table 10.4   1994 U.S. Information Technology (IT) Salaries by Location

	National Average	Wash., D.C.	Boston	New York	Florida	Chicago	Texas	Los Angeles	San Francisco
CIO/VP	$111,495	$99,000	$112,679	$109,265	$92,095	$103,460	$103,500	$153,385	$113,583
Director	$76,380	$73,805	$83,184	$70,519	$68,730	$74,818	$71,957	$84,526	$86,898
Manager/Supervisor	$57,246	$55,709	$59,625	$57,080	$49,678	$57,058	$49,248	$62,562	$65,440
Application Development Manager	$61,006	$59,052	$67,792	$58,773	$55,071	$57,397	$54,712	$65,341	$69,962
Application Designer	$51,408	$58,000	$53,300	$48,389	$46,815	$44,686	$45,688	$55,526	$58,760
Application Developer	$47,210	$47,080	$53,364	$45,055	$42,092	$41,360	$41,011	$51,242	$52,085
Project Manager	$55,691	$55,453	$63,345	$53,058	$50,065	$52,364	$53,904	$56,731	$58,541
Project Leader	$52,667	$51,138	$68,727	$47,278	$45,927	$49,925	$46,456	$56,263	$55,034
Senior Systems Analyst	$49,621	$50,250	$59,683	$48,406	$43,172	$47,301	$44,263	$50,297	$53,697
Systems Analyst	$42,166	$40,926	$47,545	$41,532	$35,795	$41,021	$38,690	$42,895	$47,990
Senior Programmer Analyst	$43,912	$43,375	$47,858	$42,136	$38,615	$40,132	$40,592	$49,249	$48,505
Programmer	$35,481	$34,693	$40,063	$33,430	$30,340	$32,905	$33,025	$40,781	$39,404
Computer Operator	$26,130	$27,056	$30,593	$23,451	$21,597	$24,095	$23,677	$29,633	$29,896
Data Entry Clerk	$20,821	$19,016	$22,250	$19,075	$17,700	$20,416	$19,430	$23,254	$23,964
Administrator	$52,508	$48,940	$64,556	$55,316	$40,738	$50,679	$45,736	$52,618	$56,691
Database Analyst	$46,410	$44,923	$55,000	$49,427	$41,838	$41,042	$40,585	$46,045	$50,687
Network Manager (LAN/WAN)	$50,466	$49,932	$55,227	$51,400	$43,740	$50,267	$44,749	$50,981	$54,704
LAN Manager	$45,460	$43,494	$51,345	$43,826	$39,865	$43,094	$44,081	$47,574	$49,059
Network Engineer	$42,471	$39,917	$44,000	$40,714	$38,231	$43,364	$38,463	$42,760	$49,253
Help Desk Manager	$42,624	$38,000	$41,572	$42,138	$40,027	$40,973	$38,350	$43,840	$51,926
Technical Support Analyst	$36,559	$33,126	$40,828	$33,943	$35,729	$38,366	$35,602	$36,567	$39,323
Computer Hardware Engineer	$39,638	$34,200	$39,143	$39,074	$39,700	$37,692	$36,033	$40,643	$48,866
PC Technician	$31,614	$27,696	$35,909	$29,847	$29,259	$31,160	$29,413	$32,188	$36,902

plans, employee stock ownership or stock purchase plans, and profit-sharing plans. Job applicants must evaluate benefit packages to compute total compensation.

Compensation is not the only factor important to computer professionals. It may not be the most important factor in many cases. Such factors as the challenge of being on the cutting edge, the opportunity to use new technology, a humanistic managerial style, and promotion from within with no barriers all have great appeal. Training and career development are vital to information professionals if they are to stay in touch technically and advance. There is significant value in training and development opportunities provided by firms. A high growth need and passion for technology are characteristic of information professionals. Unable to reward workers with promotion as in the past because of the flat organizational structure, managers are attempting to use challenge and participatory management to motivate them.

It is very important for those entering the job market to investigate companies thoroughly and to ask probing questions during the job interview. Chapters 11 and 12 will provide sources of information and job-seeking hints.

RESOURCES FOR COMPUTER AND INFORMATION PROFESSIONALS

Computer and telecommunications fields are among the most dynamic of any careers. New computer hardware, software, and communications devices are entering the market continuously. Competition both inside and outside the computer industry has made the availability of resources extremely important to computer professionals. First of all, there is tremendous pressure on these individuals to stay technologically current. A computer professional can become technologically obsolete in three to five years unless a concerted effort is made to avoid it. Some ways to avoid obsolescence include attending technical seminars, reading publications in the field, and enrolling in college classes. In addition to the pressure to keep current, computer professionals as a group have a very high growth need. This is exhibited by active involvement in the numerous professional organizations and a willingness to become involved in advanced study. The purpose of this chapter is to make the reader aware of the numerous resources at his or her disposal to use either in preparing for a computer career or in developing a career beyond the entry level. Five major areas of resources will be described and a number of specific resources listed. These areas are: computer periodicals and professional journals, professional organizations, certification, education, and training. A wealth of career information can also be acquired electronically through networks and databases.

PERIODICALS AND PROFESSIONAL JOURNALS

Computer periodicals and professional journals are excellent sources of general information. They differ in degree of technical depth. Some are written more for information managers and are more applications-oriented such as *Datamation* and *Information Systems.* Others are written for those in engineering and electronics such as *Computer Design* and *Solid State Technology.* There are hundreds of periodicals published today in the area of computer technology and its applications. To see this impressive list, consult *Ulrich's International Periodicals Directory* in the reference section of the library. It is published annually by R.R. Bowker Company, New York and London.

A good many computer periodicals can be found in public and university libraries. Most computer professionals subscribe to a number of periodicals written for their specific area of employment. Although it is often possible to identify for whom a publication is written by its name, this is not always the case.

The following is a short list of well-known periodicals, the group of computer professionals for whom they are written, and their addresses. Much of the information in this book was obtained from these publications.

> *BYTE*—personal computer owners
> BYTE Publications, Inc.
> One Phoenix Mill Lane
> Peterborough, NH 03458

> *Client Server News*—information professionals
> G–2 Computer Intelligence, Inc.
> Box 7, 3 Maple Place
> Glen Head, NY 11545–0007

> *Communications Technology*—information professionals
> Phillips Business Information, Inc.
> 1201 Seven Locks Road
> Potomac, MD 20854

> *Computer Design*—designers and engineers
> PennWell Publishing Co.
> 10 Tara Boulevard, Fifth floor
> Nashua, NH 03062–2801

> *Computer Graphics World*—computer graphics professionals
> PennWell Publishing Co.
> 10 Tara Boulevard, Fifth floor
> Nashua, NH 03602–2801

> *Systems and Network Integration*—systems personnel,
>   engineers, manufacturers
> CMP Publications, Inc.
> 600 Community Drive
> Manhasset, NY 11030

> *Computer Security Journal*—computer security professionals
> Computer Security Institute
> 600 Harrison Street
> San Francisco, CA 94107

Computerworld—everyone interested in computers
Computerworld, Inc.
375 Cochituate Road
Framington, MA 01701–9171

Corporate Computing—corporate computer executives
Ziff Davis Publishing Co.
950 Tower Lane, Nineteenth floor
Foster City, CA 94404

Data Base Management—database professionals
Auerbach Publishers
One Penn Plaza
New York, NY 10119

Data Communications—computer network professionals
McGraw–Hill, Inc.
1221 Avenue of the Americas
New York, NY 10020

Datamation—information processing professionals
Cahners Publishing Co.
275 Washington Street
Newton, MA 02158–1630

Digital News & Review—computer manufacturers and dealers
Cahners Publishing Co.
275 Washington Street
Newton, MA 02158–1630

Chilton's ECN Electronic Component News—design engineers
Chilton Co.
Chilton Way
Radnor, PA 19089

EDN Products & Careers—electronics engineers, product
    designers, systems designers
Cahners Publishing Co.
275 Washington Street
Newton, MA 02158

IEEE Network—engineers
Institute of Electrical and Electronics Engineers
345 East 47th Street
New York, NY 10017–2394

Information Systems—information processing professionals
Hitchcock Publishing Co.
191 South Gary Avenue
Carol Stream, IL 60188

Information Systems Management—managers and consultants
Warren Gorham Lamont
One Penn Plaza
New York, NY 10119

Information Today—information processing professionals
Learned Information, Inc.
143 Old Marlton Pike
Medford, NJ 08055

Information Week—information professionals
CMP Publications, Inc.
600 Community Drive
Manhasset, NY 11030

InfoWorld—personal computer users and suppliers
InfoWorld Publishing
155 Bovet Road, Suite 800
San Mateo, CA 94402

Intelligent Software Strategies—artificial intelligence
    professionals
Cutter Information Corp.
37 Broadway
Arlington, MA 02174

Journal of Systems and Software—systems analysts and
    programmers
Elsevier Science Inc.
655 Avenue of the Americas
New York, NY 10010

LAN Product News—network professionals
Worldwide Videotex
Box 3273
Boynton Beach, FL 33424–3273

Managing Office Technology—information and word
    processing managers
Penton Publishing, Inc.
1100 Superior Avenue
Cleveland, OH 44114–2543

Multimedia Computing & Presentations—information
   professionals
Multimedia Computing Corp.
2105 South Bascom Avenue, 300
Campbell, CA 95003–3278

Office—information and word processing professionals
Penton Publishing Co.
1100 Superior Avenue
Cleveland, OH 44114

Solid State Technology—device and circuit manufacturers
PennWell Publishing Co.
10 Tara Boulevard, Fifth floor
Nashua, NH 03062–2801

Telecommunications Reports—telecommunications specialists
Telecommunications Reports
1333 H Street NW, Second floor
Washington, DC 20005

PROFESSIONAL ORGANIZATIONS

Participation in professional organizations is very beneficial to computer
professionals. The organizations provide an opportunity for personal communications among members. In addition, a tremendous amount of current
information is disseminated through advanced training and seminars and the
publication of journals sponsored by the organizations. Students are encour-
aged to participate in professional associations. The price of membership for
students is greatly reduced in most cases. A good source for names and addresses of professional organizations is the *Encyclopedia of Associations,*
which is published annually and found in the reference section of the library.
Information includes names, addresses, and phone numbers of professional
associations; the date they were founded; the number of current members; a
description of the membership; publications, if any; and so on.

   The following is a list of associations and their addresses. Although it is
by no means complete, this list provides sources of information in computer
fields for both prospective and established computer professionals over a
wide range of interest areas.

American Association for Artificial Intelligence
445 Burgess Drive
Menlo Park, CA 94025

American Electronics Association
P.O. Box 54990
Santa Clara, CA 95054–0990

American Society of Information Science (newsletter of career information and job openings)
8720 Georgia Avenue, Suite 501
Silver Spring, MD 20910–3602

Association for Information and Image Managers
1100 Wayne Avenue, Suite 1100
Silver Spring, MD 20910

Association of Computer Professionals
9 Forest Drive
Plainview, NY 11803

Association for Computers and the Humanities
Humanities Research Center
Brigham Young University
2054 JKHB
Provo, UT 84602

Association for Computing Machinery (resume databank for members)
1515 Broadway
New York, NY 10036–5701

Association for Information and Image Management
1100 Wayne Avenue, Suite 1100
Silver Spring, MD 20910

Association of Independent Information Professionals
203 Pinehurst Road
Canyon, CA 94516

Association for Systems Management
1435 West Bagley Road
P.O. Box 38370
Cleveland, OH 44138–0370

Association for Women in Computing
41 Sutter Street, Suite 1006
San Francisco, CA 94104

Common
401 North Michigan Avenue
Chicago, IL 60611–4267

Computer and Automated Systems Association of SME
One SME Drive
Dearborn, MI 48128

Computer & Business Equipment Manufacturers Association
1250 Eye Street NW, Suite 200
Washington, DC 20005

Computer & Communications Industry Association
666 11th Street, NW
Washington, DC 20001

CDLA, The Computer Leasing and Remarketing Association
1212 Potomac Street, NW
Washington, DC 20007

Data Processing Management Association
505 Busse Highway
Park Ridge, IL 60068

EDP Auditors Association
3701 Algonquin Road
Rolling Meadows, IL 60008

Electronics Industries Foundation
919 18th Street NW, Suite 900
Washington, DC 20006

Independent Computer Consultants Association
933 Gardenview Office Parkway
St. Louis, Missouri 63141

IEEE Computer Society (publishes periodical with job
    openings)
1730 Massachusetts Avenue, NW
Washington, DC 20036

Information Industry Association
555 New Jersey Avenue, NW
Washington, DC 20001

Information Systems Association
920 South Waukegan Road
Lake Forest, IL 60045

Information Technology Association of America
1616 North Ft. Myer Drive, Suite 1300
Arlington, VA 22209

Institute of Electrical and Electronics Engineers (publishes
    periodical with job openings)
345 East 47th Street
New York, NY 10017

International Association for Computer Information Systems
c/o Dr. Susan Haugen
University of Wisconsin—Eau Claire
Eau Claire, WI 54702

Junior Engineering Technical Society (provides career
   information on most engineering careers)
1420 King Street, Suite 405
Alexandria, VA 22314

National Action Council for Minorities in Engineering
3 West 35th Street
New York, NY 10001

National Association of Telecommunications Officers
   & Advisors
1301 Pennsylvania Avenue, NW
Suite 600
Washington, DC 20004

National Society of Black Engineers
1454 Duke Street
P.O. Box 25588
Alexandria, VA 22313–5588

National Society of Professional Engineers
1420 King Street
Alexandria, VA 22314

National Telecommunications and Information Administration
U.S. Department of Commerce
14th & Connecticut Avenue, NW
Washington, DC 20230

Office Automation Society International
6348 Munhall Court
P.O. Box 374
McLean, VA 22101

Society for Computer Simulation International
P.O. Box 17900
San Diego, CA 92117–7900

Society for Industrial and Applied Mathematics
3600 University City Science Center
Philadelphia, PA 19104–2688

Society for Information Management
401 North Michigan Avenue
Chicago, IL 60611–4267

Society of Hispanic Professional Engineers (offers placement
    service)
5400 East Olympic Boulevard, Suite 306
Los Angeles, CA 90022

Society of Telecommunications Consultants
23123 South State Road 7, Suite 220
Boca Raton, FL 33428

Society of Women Engineers (publishes periodical with job
    openings)
120 Wall Street, Eleventh floor
New York, NY 10005

Telecommunications Industry Association
2001 Pennsylvania Avenue NW, Suite 800
Washington, DC 20006–1813

Women in Information Processing
Lock Box 39173
Washington, DC 20016

World Computer Graphics Association
5201 Leesburg Pike, Suite 201
Falls Church, VA 22041

CERTIFICATION

The Institute for Certification of Computer Professionals (ICCP) is a non-profit organization that tests and certifies computer programmers and data processing managers. The certification process is a coordinated industrywide effort to promote higher standards of performance. Currently, there are two major certification programs: the Certified Computing Professional (CCP), a professional-level title, and the Associate Computer Professional (ACP), an entry-level one. To receive either the CCP or the ACP, one must pass examinations and accept the ICCP codes of ethics, conduct, and good practice. Professionals must be recertified every three years. For specific information concerning certification, write:

Institute for Certification of Computer Professionals
2200 East Devon Avenue, Suite 268
Des Plaines, IL 60018

This certification procedure has been in existence for over twenty-five years, but not without some controversy. The ICCP certification has been criticized for emphasizing broad, general knowledge rather than specific, emerging technologies. Novell Inc. has offered technical training, testing, and certification for the designation of Certified NetWare Administrator, Certified NetWare Engineer (CNE), or Enterprise CNE. To obtain a CNE certificate, one must attend a 2–day seminar and pass a series of exams. As of May 1994, more than 35,000 professionals held CNEs, increasing by 2,200 per month on average. Some organizations require candidates for LAN manager positions to have a CNE certificate. Other vendors have begun to offer certification programs as well.

Leading individuals in information systems careers and professional associations desire to establish the professionalism in their field as has been done in other professions such as law, medicine, and accounting. They are willing to spend time and energy to develop standards of performance and good practice. Some professional groups concerned with standardizing software development processes and certifying professionals are the Canadian Standards Association, the American National Standards Institute, and the Technical Committee on Software Engineering of the IEEE Computer Society. These groups have set some widespread standards for the information systems industry. The Canadian Information Processing Society (CIPS) and the International Programmers Guild certify qualified professionals that adhere to set standards.

EDUCATION

In response to the demand for skilled computer professionals, numerous programs are available in every state. Depending on an individual's career goal, the required background may be gained in a high school, vocational school, data processing school, community college, college, or university. Educational requirements have been discussed throughout the book as part of the specific job descriptions, so this chapter will focus on where to obtain this needed education and training.

Today children as young as two years old are exposed to computers in preschools. New electronic learning aids help students become very comfortable with the new technologies. More elementary and secondary schools are offering computer literacy courses, and programming and word processing courses are being offered at the high school level as well. The first programming course is often a good determinant of whether an individual has an aptitude and a strong enough interest to pursue an information processing career. Often performance in a programming course is a better indicator of aptitude and interest than a data processing aptitude test. Since knowing how to use a computer is valuable in any career, the sooner students are exposed to them, the better. For those who can afford a home computer, there are many manufacturer-sponsored discount programs often accompanied by free introductory training courses. Early exposure to computers is helpful, but success in educational programs in computer and information fields depends on strong basic skills in language and math.

Vocational and technical schools offer a variety of programs for those interested in data entry, operations, maintenance, service, electronics, programming, and so on. Usually, specialized data-processing schools offer programs in these areas as well. At the community college, one- or two-year programs in data entry, programming, or computer operations are usually offered. Often credits can be transferred to a college offering four-year degree programs. Employers may pay for the additional education. The majority of the careers discussed in this book require college and university degrees and, in some cases, graduate study.

Probably the most useful source of educational information on programs nationwide is *The College Blue Book*. This five-volume set is particularly useful to those seeking highly specialized programs. The volume entitled "Occupational Education" includes a list—organized alphabetically by state or by subject area—of available programs of study in technical schools and community colleges. Programs to prepare individuals for technical and semiprofessional jobs such as computer electro-mechanics, operations, programming, and maintenance are included in this volume. Another volume, "Degrees Offered by College and Subject," includes degree programs such as computer science, computer systems, and information systems that are offered by two-year colleges, four-year colleges, and universities. Other volumes offer narrative descriptions of schools, costs, accreditation, enrollment figures, scholarships, fellowships, grants, loans, and a lot of other information.

The College Blue Book is found in the reference section of the library along with many other educational resources. Also available in most college and university libraries is a variety of college catalogs enabling one to compare curricula of different schools offering the degree or program of interest. Since many programs have similar titles but very different course offerings, one cannot rely on title alone when choosing a program. When "computer science" is listed, the implication is that a program will be more technical in nature. On the other hand, "information systems" usually indicates a business applications orientation. Over one hundred universities offer both undergraduate and graduate programs with a concentration in information systems. This number will rise as more companies hire business majors in positions for which technical majors would have been hired in the past.

Education is an important and expensive item. A person should shop for it the way he or she would for any other important, expensive item. Gaining information from counselors, teachers, local colleges and universities, people working in computer fields, and potential employers is advisable before selecting an educational program.

Before entering a program, the school's accreditation should be established. The national bodies that accredit these schools are:

- National Association of Trade and Technical Schools
- National Home Study Council
- Accreditation Board for Engineering and Technology

- Association of Independent Colleges and Schools
- American Association of Collegiate Schools of Business.

TRAINING

Training is the most important ingredient in the success formula for computer professionals. It is the lack of good training and development opportunities that causes individuals to become dead-ended early in their careers. The first question that a job applicant should ask is, "What kind of training and development will the company provide me if I accept this position?" The recent emphasis on training is due in part to the failure of college curricula in computer and information sciences to educate graduates in the high demand skill areas. Dramatic changes in technology and organizational structure require constant educational program evaluation and modification. Curriculum change occurs too slowly. Along with the companies specializing in training services, major computer vendors such as IBM and Wang offer seminars and institutes for all technical levels. As mentioned earlier, training opportunities also are available to members through their professional organizations.

To meet training needs, some companies are allowing employees to select the pace of training that takes place both inside and outside the work environment. This partnership enables ambitious employees to have more control over training opportunities and to advance at their own rate. In addition to the traditional stand-up lecture, company training programs will employ more educational technologies such as interactive video, computer-based training, television courses, and numerous others. The trend today, particularly with the restructuring occurring in many organizations, is toward more company-sponsored training and development programs. But going to work for a company that offers its employees a good amount of training is only part of one's growth. Staying aware of opportunities for advanced training outside the company also is important. Whether a company uses the type of partnership arrangement described above or a standard approach to training, a person is responsible for his or her own training and career development. By joining professional organizations as a student, you can take advantage of some early training opportunities and gain a competitive edge.

THE BEST RESOURCE

A person is his or her own best resource. By using good judgment in choosing and planning a career, by gaining information from a variety of sources, and by relying on well-formulated questions as well as intuition in accepting a job, an individual can increase the chances of success in a computer career. Chapter 12 includes some tips on finding a good job.

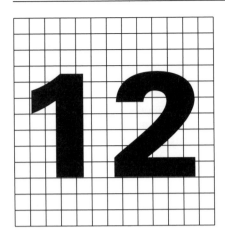

BEGINNING A SUCCESSFUL CAREER

The abundance of jobs for those with computer and information backgrounds makes finding a job easier. It has been said that anyone can find a job in information fields, but good jobs in these fields are hard to find. Changing technology causes job requirements to change as well, so graduates who have kept abreast of trends and have tailored their programs of study accordingly will be successful in finding good jobs. Experience gained through part-time jobs, internships, and involvement in campus activities will also help graduates find good jobs. Surveys of recent college graduates show that 80 percent of those seeking jobs find work within the first six months and 75 percent of these perceive their jobs to be good career starters.

All individuals do not define a "good job" in the same way; it is important for each job seeker to define what he or she wants in a job before beginning the search. For example, to the physically handicapped or to a mother with young children, a good job may be one that can be done in the home; to a student, a good job may be part-time or with flexible working hours; to a partner in a dual career marriage, a good job may be one available locally; to the technically-oriented, a good job may be one offering a number of advanced technical levels beyond entry; to an ambitious woman, a good job may be one in a company employing women managers in key positions; and so on. The job market in computer fields is open enough to accommodate many types of job requirements. However, it is very important for job seekers to have their individual requirements and career goals clearly in mind and to have prepared themselves properly.

GAINING VALUABLE EXPERIENCE

In general, employers in information fields regard the possession of specific skills as a more important qualification than educational background. Such skills as written and verbal communications, work experience, and knowledge both of the functions of the business and the technology used in the company are very important. This is not to say that grade-point average and course work are not scrutinized also. The point is that most employers care more about what you can do for their company than what you know, so in both the resume and the interview, job seekers should focus on the skills they possess and the value of these skills to the company. College students can gain marketable experience through internships, cooperative programs, and part-time jobs.

Internships and Cooperative Programs

Traditional internships are usually three-month positions, while cooperative programs (co–ops) last a college quarter, semester, or longer. Internships are sometimes arranged by an interested faculty and a company manager, and the intern is not always paid. Co–ops, on the other hand, are part of an ongoing college program for which students receive both credit and pay. These distinctions aren't as clear anymore because companies want to keep interns for longer periods, and they frequently offer paid internships. Many organizations ultimately hire their brightest interns and co–op students. Roughly 26 percent of 1993 graduates were hired from internships or co–op programs.

Smart students start looking for internships their freshman year and competition can be stiff. Professors, older students who have had internships, and family contacts in a student's chosen field can be great sources of information and referral. Interviews for internships are essentially job interviews in that students should learn everything they can about a company prior to the interview. The suggestions in this chapter may help with this, as well as the resources listed in Chapter 11. Often interview sign-up sheets are posted on campus bulletin boards. The best time slots are first, last, or right after lunch—never right before. Internships are also advertised in campus newspapers and such books as *Internships, the Guide to On-the-Job Training Opportunities for Students and Adults,* published by Peterson's Guides, Princeton, NJ. In addition, professional associations may offer information on internships available from their member companies. Fortunate students with computer or telecommunications skills and interests land internships with such companies as Apple Computer, Inc., Boeing Co., and Intel Corp.

Part-Time Jobs

Apart from intern and co–op programs, many students find part-time jobs on their own that offer both pay and experience. Though these jobs often pay minimum wage, this work experience is very important to prospective employers. Former employers can give important recommendations for full-time jobs after graduation. That an individual is reliable, works well with co-workers, and has initiative is what any prospective employer wants to hear. Many on-campus jobs can be obtained through student financial aid and job placement services. On every college campus are job boards and campus newspapers listing job openings. Graduate assistantships are available to qualified students. Computer and information majors will get more than their share of these positions if they can show expertise with computers and communications technology even though some part-time jobs will be data entry. Any opportunity for work experience prior to graduation should be considered because of the strength it lends to the job search for that first, very important, full-time job.

FINDING A GOOD JOB

It is important for each job seeker to define what he or she wants in a job before beginning the search. Individual career goals should give direction to the job search and should be well-articulated. Also, they are usually discussed in job interviews.

Locating Jobs

The task of finding a good job is twofold in that seekers must identify both companies with existing openings and companies for whom they would like to work. The fact that a company does not have an advertised opening does not mean that the company would not create an opening for an outstanding applicant. This makes the job search more complicated, but it also offers the seeker somewhat broader horizons. Students should build a network of family, friends, and associates who can refer them to others who might be able to help them locate potential openings.

Many maintain that the way to find excellent jobs is through direct contact with the person who has the authority to hire. One of the best and most widely-used books on the subject of jobfinding is *What Color Is Your Parachute?* by Richard Nelson Bolles. This book helps the jobseeker organize his or her time and energy and avoid tactics that rarely, if ever, pay off. Various avenues for locating job opportunities include college placement offices, published job openings, recruiting firms, and computerized search services.

The College Placement Office

Prospective college graduates should take advantage of the on-campus interviews arranged by the college placement office. Surveys of companies indicate that roughly 42 percent of their new college hires come from these interviews. They provide an opportunity for a first contact with major company representatives while still on campus. Since these companies are recruiting for current job openings and are willing to hire beginners, young job seekers should definitely take advantage of these opportunities. It is best to sign up early since the company representatives have time for only a limited number of interviews. To prepare for these interviews, individuals should review the information on file in the college placement office. This information, provided by the interviewing companies, often includes annual reports and recruitment materials from which students can glean facts about the company and the career opportunities it offers.

Published Job Openings

Job openings in computer science, information, and engineering are listed in *Peterson's Guide to Engineering, Science, and Computer Jobs, Peterson's Job Opportunities for Business and Liberal Arts Graduates, The Career Guide 1990, Career Visions, Career Employment Opportunities Directory,* and the *CPC Annual.* These books usually can be found in the career planning and placement office of most colleges and universities. They contain a tremendous amount of information, including listings of career opportunities, locations of employment, special training programs available with the companies, benefits, employer profiles, and addresses to write for further information. *Peterson's* books also contain information on the job market and numerous job-seeking hints.

The *CPC Annual* lists the occupational needs anticipated by approximately one thousand corporations and employers who normally recruit college graduates in all areas. One section of the *Annual* lists companies alphabetically and includes the phone number, the contact person, the products and services, when the company was established, the number of employees, what positions are available, and the location of the available positions. Another section of the *Annual* lists the U.S. government agency openings. The *Annual* lists positions for all areas, and it may include openings not listed in other directories. It also provides excellent information on job seeking in general, such as interviewing and resume-writing hints.

Professional journals provide another source of published job openings. Many of the computer journals devote a section near the end to advertising job openings. The *Wall Street Journal, New York Times,* and other big-city and local newspapers advertise openings, but responding to newspaper advertisements is rarely the way to obtain good jobs.

Recruiting Firms

Job opportunities are listed with recruiting firms. These firms provide needed services to both organizations and applicants. Often a sizable chunk of the first month's salary must be paid to the recruiting firm. Some organizations seeking employees assume the charges for the service. In some areas, beginners do not normally find good jobs through recruiting services or employment agencies. This is not the case in computer areas. Because of the demand and the difficulty in finding computer professionals with specific skills, excellent opportunities are listed with recruiting firms. These firms provide needed services to both organizations and job applicants.

A number of recruiting firms, such as Source EDP and Robert Half, specialize in computer careers. Both of these firms place lower-level as well as top information personnel. Other firms specialize in areas such as operations personnel, programmers and analysts, IS executives. Two well-known firms are Fox Morris Personnel Consultants and Dunhill Personnel System, Inc. These firms research the market thoroughly, and the results of their surveys are frequently published in the journal *Computerworld.* These are but a few of the many recruitment firms placing applicants in computer-related jobs.

These recruitment firms along with the companies seeking employees advertise positions in information journals.

Job fairs are held in large cities around the country in which company representatives talk to professionals about opportunities within their companies. In addition, seminars in job-seeking skills are offered. There is no charge to job seekers for either participation in the seminars or placement in jobs. To learn more about the job fairs, interested individuals may call the toll-free number 1–800–JOB–SHOW. *Computerworld* publishes an annual Campus Recruitment Edition, written for and distributed to college students.

Professional Association Placement Services

Placement services are offered by a number of professional organizations. The job seeker should become affiliated at the outset with one or more of the professional organizations for individuals in his or her area of expertise. Even associations without placement services may provide directories of their members free or at minimal cost. These associations can often recommend or supply additional sources of information. A long list of professional organizations and their addresses was included in Chapter 11.

Computerized Search Services

Computerized search services are gaining in popularity across college campuses. The services vary from school to school but may include some of those listed here. Students may call up a list of job openings in their chosen fields. Some systems place student resumes on-line for companies to review. Other systems allow students to sign up for on-campus interviews by computer. *The 1995 National Job Hotline Directory* offers information organized by state (including some Canada listings) that enables job seekers to access more than 3,000 employment hotlines 24 hours a day.

Search for jobs and career information via the Internet. Those with a full Internet connection and a browser can access the *Interactive Employment Network* or the *Internet Business Directory*. In general, the networks offer the most jobs for those in high-technology areas. *Datamation Databank* is a resume database primarily for data-processing and engineering professionals. There is no cost and it currently has between 600 and 700 clients. Most other resume databases charge for their services. Some of these are *Career Net Online, Job Bank USA, National Employee Database,* and *HispanData,* designed for Hispanic professionals. The *Job-Seeker's Guide to On-Line Resources* is a 64-page paperback listing resume databases, job-posting services, and other on-line resources. It may be found in college libraries or can be purchased for $14.95 plus $4 shipping by writing:

Kennedy Publications
Fizwilliam, NH 03447

GAINING COMPANY INFORMATION

It is very important for an individual to have knowledge about the specific companies for which he or she will be interviewing.

Computer Journals

The best way to gain information about what is happening in the computer industry and in companies with large computer installations is by reading journals for computer professionals. A list of key computer journals was provided in Chapter 11. Along with advertised openings, these journals provide a wealth of information to help the job seeker ask timely and well-informed questions during the interview and make a final decision on what company would be the best employer.

Key journals such as *Datamation* conduct industry surveys annually and publish the results. For example, *Datamation* ranks the top one hundred companies in the computer industry in a number of ways. Overall rankings are based on total data processing revenues for the previous year. Also reported are the percentage growth rate, return on equity, and profiles and addresses for all the top one hundred companies. In addition, industry segments are analyzed. Percentage growth of the segments is reported along with the top producers of data communications equipment, personal computers, mainframes, processing services, peripherals, and other equipment. The top companies spending research and development dollars, adding employees, cutting back employees, gaining ground on the stock market, and losing ground on the stock market also are listed. This type of industry information is extremely valuable to the job seeker.

Published Information on Companies and Industries

Numerous sources of information offering general information about companies are available in most university libraries. The current *U.S. Industrial Outlook* analyzes two hundred industries with projections into the future. It is published by the Bureau of Industrial Economics of the U.S. Department of Commerce and can be found in the government documents section of the library. Standard & Poor's surveys of industries include current and basic analyses for the major domestic industries. The current analysis includes latest industry developments; industry, market, and company statistics; and appraisals of investment outlook. The basic analysis includes prospects for the particular industry; an analysis of trends and problems; spotlights on major segments of the industry; growth in sales and earnings of leading companies in the industry; and other information over a ten-year span. Another excellent source of up-to-date industry information is *The Value Line Investment Survey.*

Many sources focus on specific companies. The *Dun & Bradstreet Directories, Moody's Manuals,* and *Thomas's Register* all provide specific company information; such as the address and phone number of the company, what the business produces, its annual sales, and the names of officers and directors. If an individual is interested in the backgrounds of those who make it to the top in a particular company, *Standard & Poor's Register of Corporations, Directors, and Executives* and *Dun & Bradstreet's Reference Book of Corporate Managements* both provide this type of information. Two excellent sources on the computer industry are *The Computer Industry Almanac* and *The Information Industry Directory.* These resources are found in the reference section in public and college libraries. Annual and quarterly corporate reports are usually housed in the college career placement offices.

Computerized Information on Companies

If gathering information quickly is necessary, use the computer. With a few dollars and a little help from the college librarian, a student can research companies using the computer by searching *Disclosure,* a database of all U.S. headquartered companies that trade stock publicly. Within seconds, annual and quarterly reports will appear. Other databases include *Dun & Bradstreet's Millions Dollar Directory, Dun's Market Identifiers, Trinet U.S. Business, Standard & Poor's Corporate Register, Moody's Corporate Profiles,* and *Moody's Corporate News.*

Information on companies can be used by the job seeker to prepare a list of possible employers to contact; to eliminate companies with low growth potential; to identify a job target for the resume; and to compile a list of intelligent questions that will impress any interviewer.

The Resume

The first contact that most individuals have with a company is the resume. The resume has to be good or a job applicant may never gain an interview. Every statement should show how an applicant is qualified for the position he or she seeks. As a reflection of one's skill in written communication it is a perfect way to bias the interviewer in an applicant's behalf before he or she walks through the door. A resume is basically a sales device. It should do three things. First, it should emphasize the most positive features in an individual's background, such as maintaining an A average in college. Second, it should stress positive contributions to organizations in the past, such as implementation of a successful system. Finally, it should describe positive personal attributes and abilities, such as possessing excellent user interface skills. The best resumes are written by individuals themselves rather than professional resume-preparation services. Only individuals can present themselves in their best light and sound truthful doing it. It is wise, however, to get some editorial help from a career counselor or other skilled individual, since the resume should be the best possible.

The following are some basic hints for writing a good resume:

1. People usually skim resumes. Too many numbers, too much verbiage, poor spacing, and unclear headings all make a resume difficult to skim.

2. No matter how terrific a person is or how much experience he or she has had, a resume should be no longer than two pages. A person should only use a third page after excluding information such as health, marital status, number of children, and hobbies. Although unnecessary, these items may be included on a scanty resume but should never be the reason for an additional page. One should stick to the facts and save philosophy for the interview if asked about it. Unnecessary words such as "I," "he," or "she" should be eliminated. Resumes are usually written in phrases—not complete sentences.

3. Action words such as "coordinated," "supervised," and "developed" should be used. A resume should be oriented toward results and accomplishments rather than duties. The tone should be as positive as the content.

4. The resume should be free of spelling or grammatical errors and neatly typed or professionally printed on white or ivory rag paper. No fancy typesetting or binders should be used.

5. Salaries, reasons for termination, references, supervisors' names, politics, religion, race, ethnic background, sex, height, weight, and pictures should be excluded.

6. An individually-typed cover letter should be used each time a resume is sent to a prospective employer. In it the applicant introduces himself or herself, explains the reason for writing, describes potential contributions to the company, and requests an interview. A job target should be identified in the cover letter if a target resume is not used. Copies of all letters sent should be kept in one file folder; responses requiring action by the applicant should be held in a second; and rejection letters should be kept in a third. Whenever possible, the letter should be addressed to a specific person rather than to a title such as "Personnel Director."

With the above basics clearly in mind, the applicant should write a resume that is a summary of his or her education, work experience, interests, career goals, and any other information that qualifies that individual for the position sought. An excellent book on resume writing is *Resumes for College Students and Recent Graduates,* published in 1994 by VGM Career Horizons, NTC Publishing Group, 4255 W. Touhy Avenue, Lincolnwood, IL 60646–1975.

There are different formats that may be used in developing a resume. A commonly-used format is a chronological arrangement of educational and work experiences, each listed separately with the most recent experience first. If an applicant is seeking a job that is a natural progression from former jobs and has a good work history with growth and development, this is a good format to use. However, if an applicant's former work history consists of part-time jobs while in college, there is a better format: the functional arrangement.

A resume organized around functional or topical headings stresses competencies. Such headings as "Research" and "Programming" enable an individual to include course work, special projects, and work experience in these areas. These headings are geared to the type of position the applicant is seeking. Actual work experience is included at the bottom of the resume. Both functional and chronological resumes can be used for broad career objectives.

Another type of resume used widely today is the targeted resume. Jobs have become more specific and highly defined than they used to be. Changing technology has caused the creation of many new, specialized positions. Beginners who are aware of the job market will have developed some special areas of expertise in order to make them viable applicants for some of these new specialized positions. The job target is clearly stated along with specific areas of expertise related to the applicant's ability to do the job.

Which resume format is best is a function of the applicant's experience and career objectives. A standard resume prepared by an applicant for a career in information systems could be composed something like the following:

Name

Address

Phone

Target Job or Personal Objectives
(The description under "Target Job" will be highly specific, while the one under "Personal Objectives" will be broad enough to cover a range of employment possibilities.)

Education
(Beginning with most recent experience, this includes colleges or technical schools, degrees, date received, and major areas of study.)

Technical Expertise
(Such areas as systems analysis, design, programming, feasibility studies, user training, and so on should be included.)

Hardware/Software
(Specific hardware and software used should be listed.)

Experience
(Dates, job titles, activities, accomplishments, and levels of authority should be included.)

The above resume format might also include outside interests or a positive comment such as, "I am considered systematic and results-oriented and work effectively as part of a team." Note that a chronological arrangement would merely list areas of expertise and hardware and software used under the headings "Technical Expertise" and "Hardware/Software." It would describe them in more detail in the section entitled "Experience." A functional approach would expand the sections "Technical Expertise" and "Hardware/Software", listing courses, assistantships, internships, and so on, and would abbreviate the "Experience" section if the paid work experience was outside the desired area of work. Such accomplishments as published articles in related fields, business and educational honors, and accreditations and licenses—for example, a Certificate in Data Processing—would strengthen the resume and should be included. References should not be listed on the resume but should be provided when requested on the company's job application form.

A good resume increases the likelihood that an individual will be contacted for an interview. This contact is often by phone, so the job seeker should keep a pad and pen beside the phone to record any information from such calls. The more organized and in control an applicant appears, the more impressed prospective employers will be.

For specialized help in resume writing in computer fields, a new book, *Winning Resumes for Computer Personnel* by Anne doSola Cardoza, is available from Barron's.

PREPARING FOR THE INTERVIEW

Preparing for a job interview involves a lot more than putting on clothes. An earlier section described sources of information on specific companies. It sometimes is possible for an individual to obtain a schedule of his or her visit to the company in advance, including the names and titles of the interviewers. If any are senior managers, their backgrounds could be researched in an industry *Who's Who* or one of the earlier sources mentioned, and some aspect of this background could be casually referred to during the interview. A job candidate also could request a sample copy of any standard employee newsletter, relevant company publication, or an annual company stockholder report.

Applicants for positions in computer fields should be prepared to discuss technical equipment and procedures, the computer industry as a whole, and career goals and methods for achieving them. Since the applicant has some time during the interview process to ask questions, it is best to have developed a list of critical questions, some based on the pre-interview research. Examples of such questions include the following:

- What type of performance appraisal system is used?
- How is the company's career development system set up, and what are some common career paths within the company?

- How are new workers trained and developed?
- How long has the prospective supervisor held that position?
- What is the management style of the company?
- In what direction is future growth anticipated?

In short, any information that the applicant has been unable to gain in advance that might impact heavily on his or her career development should be learned in the interview, if possible.

Conservative dress—without looking uniformed—is usually safe attire for a job interview. Women might wear a simply-tailored suit, a neat hairdo, plain jewelry, and moderate makeup and perfume. Men might wear a conservative suit, shirt, and tie. Polished shoes, trimmed and styled hair, and clean fingernails are all important.

Posture is significant, as are all types of body language. A firm handshake, eye contact, poise, ease, and manners all contribute to a positive interview. The novice job applicant might even improve his or her overall performance at a job interview by practicing beforehand in front of a mirror.

THE INTERVIEW

Each corporation has a culture of its own. An applicant's ability to fit into this culture is often the key to being hired. Sizing up the corporate culture is something an applicant can do by walking into the lobby. Is there elaborate security or a clubby atmosphere? Is the coffee served in fine china or styrofoam cups? Do the executives sometimes pick up their own phones? Are only degrees and certificates displayed in the offices, or family photos as well? The applicant's ability to pick up on the degree of formality or informality and modify interview behaviors accordingly might make the difference between a job offer or disappointment. The fact is that IS managers are not only looking for levels of experience with equipment and software, but for types of individuals that would fit comfortably into the organization. In other words, the chemistry between candidate and interviewer is critical. Both need to determine whether or not they would like to work together daily. This is a highly subjective factor.

The applicants most likely to be hired are effective communicators both on professional and personal levels. They are warm, outgoing, enthusiastic, self-confident, and have many other good qualities. Both the applicant and interviewer are under stress. However, if both can relax during the interview, the interview will be better and more information will be exchanged. The interviewer is looking at both substance, which is basically a person's past performance, and style, which includes communication skills, poise, self-confidence, and motivation. Broad questions such as "How would you describe yourself as a person?" and "How can you contribute to our organization?" reveal the applicant's values and personality and how the applicant organizes his or her thoughts. How a person fields questions also shows performance under pressure, quickness, energy, and sense of humor.

Often a preliminary interview is conducted by a member of the personnel department who is skilled in interview techniques to determine whether a candidate will fit into the corporate culture. If this interview goes well for the candidate, a second interview is conducted by the manager of the department in which the applicant would work. Sometimes a technical specialist will sit in on the interview and help with the evaluation. Applicants for programming positions are sometimes asked to take a test. Entry-level candidates are given an aptitude test which attempts to measure an individual's ability to learn. More experienced candidates are given proficiency tests to measure skills in state-of-the-art programming languages and databases. Expert-system computer tests used today, which can measure a candidate's level of understanding, reveal subtle strengths and weaknesses. Although most people cringe at the idea of tests, they in fact provide a much more objective evaluation of a candidate's ability to do a job than the subjective reactions of an interviewer.

An applicant should work in questions as the interview progresses or, if the interviewer shows a high need for structure, should wait until asked if there are any questions. The applicant's questions should emphasize professional growth and work-related activities. Such topics as salary and benefits should be discussed after the job is offered. Some bargaining then may occur, particularly if the applicant has another offer in hand.

Ironically enough, most applicants forget to ask for the job. An applicant should both ask for the job and thank the interviewer. Some indication of when the applicant will hear from the company should be given. The interest that an interviewer shows in an applicant does not mean that a job will be offered. It is standard operating procedure; the interviewer is building goodwill and keeping the applicant interested. Applicants should go on as many interviews as possible and carefully compare companies and offers, no matter how well a first interview goes or how certain an applicant is that a job will be offered. Additional offers not only provide an individual with choices but give some leverage to the applicant who can then bargain for salary and benefits.

With careful planning and preparation, individuals are bound for success in computer careers. This book is only the beginning of a lifelong experience with computers. Good jobs and interesting futures are high technology's promise to the workforce. Those who take advantage of this promise will not be disappointed.

BIBLIOGRAPHY

Appleton, Elaine L., "Staffing Up? Here's What You'll Pay," *Datamation,* October 15, 1994, 53–56.

Caminiti, Susan, "What Team Leaders Need to Know," *Fortune,* February 20, 1995, 93–100.

CPC Salary Survey, January 1995, Bethlehem PA: College Placement, Inc., 1995.

"Home Computers," *Business Week,* November 28, 1994, 88–94.

Houseman, Judy, "CNE Statues Retains High Value in Education," *Computer Reseller News,* May 30, 1994, 119–120.

Jacob, Rahul, "Corporate Reputations," *Fortune,* March 6, 1995, 54–85.

Keeton, Laura E., "Networking," *The Wall Street Journal,* February 27, 1995, R9.

Kiechel, Walter, "How We Will Work in the Year 2000," *Fortune,* May 17, 1993, 38–52.

Kleinschrod, Walter A., "Technology Careers: How High Can you Go?" *Beyond Computing,* November/December, 1994, 38–44.

Labich, Kenneth, "Kissing Off Corporate America," *Fortune,* February 20, 1995, 44–52.

"Looking Good: Where the Fast Growth Is and Will Be," *The Wall Street Journal,* February 27, 1995, R5.

Moad, Jeff, "When the Career Ladder Crumbles," *Datamation,* January 15, 1995, 44–47.

Occupational Outlook Handbook, 1994–95 ed., U.S. Department of Labor: Washington DC.

Serwer, Andrew E., "Trouble in Franchise Nation," *Fortune,* March 6, 1995, 115–129.

Smith, Lee, "Landing That First Real Job," *Fortune,* May 16, 1994, 58–60.

Stewart, Thomas A., "Planning a Career in a World Without Managers," *Fortune,* March 20, 1995, 72–80.

Sullivan, R. Lee, "The Office That Never Closes," *Forbes,* May 23, 1994, 212–213.

"The Craze for Consultants," *Business Week,* July 25, 1994, 60–66.

Toronto Globe & Mail, August 30, 1994, C1.

Turban, Gregory E., "Gender Differences in the Information Systems Managerial Ranks: An Assessment of Potential Discriminatory Practices," *MIS Quarterly,* June 1994, 129–142.

Wilde, Candee, "Seventh Annual Special Report on Pay Trends: At Last, the Gap Narrows," *Computerworld,* September 6, 1993, 91–100.

Wood, Christina, "Kiss the Office Goodbye!" *PC World,* October 1994, 143–150.

"Work & Family," *Business Week,* June 28, 1993, 80–88.

"Your Desktop in the Year 1996," *Fortune,* July 11, 1994, 86–98.

JOB INDEX

A complete list of titles in our extensive *Opportunities* series

OPPORTUNITIES IN

Accounting
Acting
Advertising
Aerospace
Airline
Animal & Pet Care
Architecture
Automotive Service
Banking
Beauty Culture
Biological Sciences
Biotechnology
Broadcasting
Building Construction Trades
Business Communication
Business Management
Cable Television
CAD/CAM
Carpentry
Chemistry
Child Care
Chiropractic
Civil Engineering
Cleaning Service
Commercial Art & Graphic
  Design
Computer Maintenance
Computer Science
Counseling & Development
Crafts
Culinary
Customer Service
Data Processing
Dental Care
Desktop Publishing
Direct Marketing
Drafting
Electrical Trades
Electronics
Energy
Engineering
Engineering Technology
Environmental
Eye Care
Farming and Agriculture
Fashion
Fast Food
Federal Government
Film
Financial

Fire Protection Services
Fitness
Food Services
Foreign Language
Forestry
Franchising
Gerontology & Aging Services
Health & Medical
Heating, Ventilation, Air
  Conditioning, and
  Refrigeration
High Tech
Home Economics
Homecare Services
Horticulture
Hospital Administration
Hotel & Motel Management
Human Resource Management
Information Systems
Installation & Repair
Insurance
Interior Design & Decorating
International Business
Journalism
Laser Technology
Law
Law Enforcement & Criminal
  Justice
Library & Information Science
Machine Trades
Marine & Maritime
Marketing
Masonry
Medical Imaging
Medical Technology
Mental Health
Metalworking
Military
Modeling
Music
Nonprofit Organizations
Nursing
Nutrition
Occupational Therapy
Office Occupations
Paralegal
Paramedical
Part-time & Summer Jobs
Performing Arts
Petroleum
Pharmacy
Photography

Physical Therapy
Physician
Physician Assistant
Plastics
Plumbing & Pipe Fitting
Postal Service
Printing
Property Management
Psychology
Public Health
Public Relations
Publishing
Purchasing
Real Estate
Recreation & Leisure
Religious Service
Restaurant
Retailing
Robotics
Sales
Secretarial
Social Science
Social Work
Special Education
Speech-Language Pathology
Sports & Athletics
Sports Medicine
State & Local Government
Teaching
Teaching English to Speakers
  of Other Languages
Technical Writing &
  Communications
Telecommunications
Telemarketing
Television & Video
Theatrical Design &
  Production
Tool & Die
Transportation
Travel
Trucking
Veterinary Medicine
Visual Arts
Vocational & Technical
Warehousing
Waste Management
Welding
Word Processing
Writing
Your Own Service Business

VGM Career Horizons
a division of *NTC Publishing Group*
4255 West Touhy Avenue
Lincolnwood, Illinois 60646–1975